A SLEW
OF
STUPID CRIMINALS

~ plus~

Some Spectacular Misspellings
and Other Atrocious Crimes

Paper Moon Publishing

Paper Moon Publishing
7230 South County Road P
Lake Nebagamon, WI 54849

A SLEW OF STUPID CRIMINALS
plus Some Spectacular Misspellings
and Other Atrocious Crimes

Printed in the United States of America by Morris Publishing
3212 E. Hwy 30 • Kearney, NE 68847 • 800-650-7888

10 9 8 7 6 5 4 3 2

Editing, Layout, Cover Design: Judith James
Cover Photo: Michael P. Savage
Copy Editing: Leslie Ione Leraan

ISBN 0-9653027-2-5
Library of Congress Card Catalog Number 96-71108

FOREWORD

During 34 years as an Assistant Ramsey County Attorney, I happened across many amusing or curious incidents, which I collected and now recount. In most instances, I have used initials or some means of disguising the names of the people to avoid embarrassment. The incidents actually occurred, mostly as written, although I have embellished some slightly in order to make the stories a little more interesting.

Some of these incidents are almost unbelievable, but they are, nonetheless, substantially true; If you don't believe it, ask yourself how anyone could possibly have made them up.

You will doubtless note, there is a high content of "gallows humor." Prosecuting criminal cases can be depressing and distressing. Perhaps the only way to maintain sanity is to see humor in what are otherwise very serious situations.

These incidents are not arranged in any particular order; I simply wrote them down randomly, as they occurred to me.

Along the way, I have read police reports numbering into the hundreds-of-thousands, and these have contained some misspellings so profound as to bring tears to my eyes, hence, the title. I have interspersed these throughout the recorded incidents. They almost never bear any relationship to the incident being recounted.

ROLAND M AND HIS GANG

Roland and two other Native Americans went to a small "ma and pa" motel, located near the outskirts of St. Paul, intent on robbing it. It had a large picture window directly opposite a picture window on the house across the street — where ma and pa lived. An alarm system had been rigged so the clerk had only to step on a foot button to alert the people in the house.

Roland and his two confederates went into the motel, guns drawn, and announced a stickup. The clerk then in charge, the granddaughter of the owners, sounded the alarm. The owners looked across the street, saw what was going on and called the police.

Meanwhile, back at the motel, the clerk gave up the money and as the robbers were about to leave, she commented, "Just a minute. I think my granddad has some more money in a safe around here, someplace. Let's see if I can find it."

Good thinking, thought Roland.

She fished around for a while and got a safe open and handed over a little more money. They were about to leave again and she announced, "If you'll wait a second more, I think there's a little more money in one of these drawers." She slammed a few drawers open and shut and came up with some more money, which she gave them.

As they were about to leave again, she said, "Oh look, a police car just drove up. Why don't you three guys hide in the closet and if they find you, we'll just say we were having a party."

Roland was impressed with her cool presence of mind, and following her suggestion, the three hid in the closet. As the police entered, she pointed to the closet door and, using her hand, signaled they had guns.

The police opened the door, guns drawn, and found the three huddled together on the floor. Roland looked up, with a gun in one hand and a sack of money in the other and said, "We were just having a party."

The party lasted 20 years.

IF AT FIRST YOU DON'T SUCCEED . . .

Once we had a guy who was bent on committing suicide, but too gutless to pull his own trigger. He implored his wife to do it for him and, notwithstanding her resistance, he finally succeeded in nagging her to the point of compliance. She made a new belly button alongside his regular one, holding the smoking gun in one hand and her nursing baby in the opposite arm. What a touching domestic scene that must have been.

The suicidal nut crawled out on the porch to pump out, not wanting to get blood all over the carpeting. Ma called the cops, who came and took him to the hospital where his miserable life was saved.

He was, however, if nothing else, determined. Following the old adage of "try, try again," he gave it another effort a few months later. On this occasion, he was driving a car on River Road in Minneapolis with his new girlfriend in the front seat (his wife, ironically enough, having been abandoned because of her ineptitude). Slamming on the brakes near the Franklin Avenue Bridge he announced his intention to jump. He ran out some distance, but still not far enough to be over the water. He then climbed the railing and pushed off. By a quirk of fate, which couldn't be duplicated again in a million years, he managed to land with both feet exactly on top of a cyclone fence. It catapulted him, more-or-less like a trampoline, into some nearby bushes. Aside from having two broken ankles, he was almost as good as new. Some losers just can't lose.

SOME FAMOUS VENTILATOR SHAFT BURGLARIES

A number of burglars seem to favor sheet metal ventilator shafts as a means of gaining ingress; they usually provide access, out of sight, through the roof and lead to an accessible part of the building. Typically one needs an accomplice to assist, usually to lower the culprit down slowly by a rope tied around the chest and, on occasion, to pull the burglar out in order to beat a hasty retreat if someone happens to be inside.

This can be hazardous, however. In one such case, the ventilator shaft was only about 20-by-20 inches. Bobby L, a very skinny burglar, attempted it. After a vertical drop of about six feet, the shaft took a horizontal run of about 12 feet and then continued vertically for about 12 feet more. Where it ended its horizontal run and resumed its last vertical drop, there was a flap of sheet metal about four inches wide across the entire bottom surface of the opening.

The culprit successfully negotiated this, as the flap was oriented downward across the entire width of the opening. He successfully got to the bottom of the last run and was about to "pop" the shaft open at a seam with his elbows, when he became alarmed because the night swamper arrived to clean the place (a bar) up. The noise the swamper made spooked Bobby, who pulled on the rope a couple of times to signal his confederate to pull him out of there.

The "ham fist" on the other end of the rope started pulling as hard and fast as he could. This particular ventilator shaft had joints every four feet. These joints were fastened with sheet metal screws spaced every six inches around the shaft, and the screws protruded about three quarters of an inch into the interior. Our erstwhile burglar friend got himself keelhauled across these screws, which tore the living tar out of his clothing and skin.

When he got up to the point where the vertical portion turned horizontal, he was pulled over the aforementioned tin flap and it bent upwards from its usual down position and pinned the culprit at about the level of his belly. There he remained trapped, with his legs hanging down and the rest of his body horizontal, while his buddy was tugging and hauling on the rope to no avail. Finally, daylight started to break and "Old Hamfist." handling the rope, hollered down the ventilator shaft that he was going to leave.

Mr. Burglar hung there until about 8:00 AM, when the employees started to arrive and heard his scritch-scratching. Thinking an animal was caught, they called the humane society. They arrived and cut the sheet metal with a pair of tin snips. The entire lower area of the shaft was red with blood.

The burglar lived to regret the episode and go to prison. Two weeks after the fact, he was one giant scab from head to foot.

* * * * *

One of St. Paul's slightly less clever criminals, Clyde M, altered the plan of attack slightly when he went down a large chimney of a meat processing plant. How he intended to break into the interior by using this technique has never been ascertained. Clyde failed to take note of the fact the chimney was smoking at the time he started down, or if he did take note, he chose to ignore whatever that meant.

Although there were iron rungs on the outside of the chimney, there were none on the inside. Clyde, aware of this for some reason (probably recent exploration), tied a rope around himself and tied the other end to the top, outside rung so he could lower himself slowly. Unfortunately, the rope was about 30 feet too short to allow him to reach the bottom.

In any case, he wound up being roasted; when he was fished out, the meat fell off the bone like a badly overdone turkey. With the passing of Clyde, the human gene pool may have been ever so slightly improved.

In remembrance of Clyde, our office initiated what came to be known as the *Clyde M Award for Extraordinary Dumbshitedness*, to be given annually to the most deserving candidate. It was awarded to Clyde posthumously.

* * * * *

Another case occurred at a fried chicken take-out clone of Colonel Sander's KFC. About a half-hour after it closed, some moron decided to burglarize it. On that occasion, our burglar friend went down a ventilator shaft which was only about eight feet long and straight down. He descended without benefit of a rope. The problem for him was, the shaft opened at the bottom about 18-inches above the still boiling french fry grease. He landed about half way up to his knees in the boiling grease.

The shaft was too low to crawl out from under and, besides, he would have had to dip himself further into the grease. It was also too slippery from accumulated grease for him to climb back out and turned out to be too strong for him to pop with his elbows.

His screams attracted passersby out in the street, who notified a cruising police car. A cop climbed on top of the building, took of his gun belt and dropped it down the shaft, using it to fish the burglar out.

It's been 500 years since boiling in oil has been an accepted punishment, but this guy did it to himself. He was a big winner of the Clyde M Award.

MAYBE HE SHOULD HAVE SHAVED

Leaving ventilator shafts, we go now to Jake D, a six-foot, six-inch slow learner who had a full head of carrot red hair with a beard to match. Jake once stuck up the liquor store where he regularly did business and was well known to the owner. To be said on Jake's behalf, it was winter and he wore a hood, which partially covered his hair, but did nothing to hide his beard.

Jake went in with his gun and demanded all the money from the till. The nonplused owner replied, "What's going on, Jake, is this some kind of a joke?"

Slowly, and after a great deal of careful thought, Jake replied, "Duh, I'm not Jake — stick 'em up."

The owner had little choice but to comply and Jake helped himself to the till, taking both bills and change. He then took two bottles of the brand of liquor he habitually ordered, one for each pocket of the jacket. He trudged out the door and into the freshly fallen snow.

The store manager called the police and reported the direction Jake went, along with Jake's description, which was unnecessary, as nearly every cop in town knew him. He was caught within a block-and-a-half and returned to the store, his pockets still bulging with the money and liquor bottles.

The owner positively identified him and added, "Hey, make him turn around once so I can see his back." When Jake was turned, the owner exclaimed, "Yep, his hip pocket was turned inside out when he was in here moments ago, just like it is now."

Jake quickly shoved the pocket back in and added, "It wasn't either."

Another Clyde M winner.

* * * * *

Jake had one other humorous run-in with the law. A citizen walking down Rice Street in St. Paul, saw a wrecking truck driving down the street and noticed this very large guy with bright red hair driving. The tow cable was hooked up to a safe, which struck the guy as unusual. He got the license number when it stopped at a red light and called the police. They immediately recognized Jake's description and went to the garage where he lived.

There they found Jake, draped over the safe, sound asleep. A camera car was called and photos were taken, after which they woke Jake up.

Never sleep on the job.

I promised some spectacular misspellings so, here's the first one.

~

A *loan* female was seated in the car.

Makes you wonder who they loaned her out to.

~

STAR WITNESS

The finest witness I have ever encountered was one Marion M, and older, portly, black male who always lived at (although claiming no proprietary interest in) what might most generously be described as a gambling-tippling-whorehouse. Marion did not want trouble at his place as that brought the police. Whenever anyone caused trouble, Marion came to court and put the finger on that person in a very indelible way. Two cases in which he testified come quickly to mind.

The first one was a simple shooting of one patron by another. The origins of the dispute have dissipated into the mists of time. In any event, Marion was in the kitchen frying chicken wings (at 2:00 AM). Suddenly, a shot rang out and in his words, "I just ran out there to see what them boys was doing. I heard a scuffle and a shot and I just wanted to know what was going on. I had no idea they was gambling out there. If I'd a known that, I would have told 'em to cut it out; we can't have none of that funny stuff around here."

Continuing (Marion never had to be asked more than one question — "Tell us what happened, Marion?") "I looked over and here was this one poor boy, lyin' on the floor, bleeding from his leg. I don't know what happened, but this other gentleman, sittin' at the table over there (indicating the alleged shooter), he was standing there with a gun in his hand, and you know what he did?"

At this point, Marion simulated a gun with his hand and pointed finger. "He just raised his gun up to his mouth like this and blew the smoke out of the end of the barrel," Marion said, blowing on the end of his finger. "Then he looked at down at this poor boy who was shot and just smiled."

Marion flashed a big, wide grin and finished, "But I don't know what happened." The jury did.

* * * * *

The other case with Marion as a witness came when Jessie James C, also known as Tex, shot and killed Joe M, one of the town's principal pimps. Again, gambling was involved (all ostensibly without Marion's knowledge or consent), this time down in the basement.

Tex lost $20 and Joe refused to allow him to play further as he ran out of credit. "How much do I owe?" asked Tex.

"Twenty dollars," replied Joe.

"How long do I have to get it and get back in the game?" Tex wanted to know.

"One half-hour," Joe answered.

Tex left and returned in a half-hour and asked, "How much time is left?"

"Your time is up," replied Joe, consulting a large, gold pocket watch.

"No motherfucker, your time is up!" Tex drew his trusty pistol and started blazing away, hitting no one.

Any number of folks, including Joe, jumped up from the table and started a stampede. One tipped over a 50-gallon barrel which contained mostly garbage, and also, for some unexplained reason, a few gallons of blue paint. The paint spilled and everyone tracked it all over the floor. There were blue footprints throughout the basement, but mostly in the men's room where everyone, including Joe, took refuge.

Tex hollered through the bathroom door, "Send him out or I'm shooting through the door."

Upon hearing this disquieting news, several of Joe's best friends told him he was going to have to leave now. They pushed him out the door where he was met with a fusillade of shots. Joe staggered up the stairs and out into the backyard, where he fell.

At this point, Marion told the rest of the story. "I was in the kitchen frying chicken wings (again at 2:00 AM). I had no idea they was gambling down there. I heard a ruckus and shouting and shots fired. I heard running up the back stairs and looked out the back. Poor Joe staggered out the back door and fell in the yard. The man they call Tex, sittin' right there at the table, he ran out and stood over Joe."

"Joe, he just looked up and said, 'Why? Why did this have to happen?' Tex, he had a pistol in his hand and he leaned over and slapped Joe alongside the head with it and put it up to his head and said, 'You just lie there and die, motherfucker,' but I don't know what happened."

Joe died wearing a big choker diamond ring on each of his fingers and thumbs. His estate was probated on the spot, mostly by his friends from the bathroom. His women were also evenly distributed among his associates, who, in some cases, put them in the trunks of their cars and drove off.

* * * * *

Tex was involved in another shooting at a place called the Turtle Club. He was painting the ceiling when an associate from Chicago was importuning him to go to The Windy City with him. Tex declined, continuing to stand on his ladder and paint.

After a time his friend commented, "Well, okay. I'll tell your mother that I saw you, but that you were dead." With that, Tex's friend shot him in the back, but it didn't kill him — or even wound him very bad. They left the bullet in his back.

~

After we apprehended the culprit, we returned to the scene for a *minuet*.

How dainty that must have been.

~

BAD AIM

Another shooting which impressed me occurred, again, at a gambling-tippling-whorehouse when Wallace W arrived. Following his customary habit upon entry into a crowded room, he drew his trusty .44 and started waving it around in a threatening manner just to impress folks. One habitué took alarm and drew his own gun and ducked behind his close friend, Foster N — to use him as a shield. He then raised his gun to shoot Wallace, but instead got Foster in the back of the head at a distance of three inches. Imagine his chagrin. It was a case of the most horse-shit hand-eye coordination I've ever encountered.

~

The victim (of rape) was lying nude on the ground, so I used a towel to cover her *waste*.

~

DO AS MUCH AS YOU CAN

Livinia S was an 80-year-old, cancer-ridden widow who was buying an old, beat-up house which was heavily mortgaged. To make ends meet, she rented out rooms to people for about $10 a week. A 20-year-old, ne'er-do-well moved in on her. At first he slept on the porch, but later, when it started to turn cold, moved into her bed with her. He was about the most shiftless jerk you could hope to meet, and he constantly stole her desperately needed money to go buy beer or dope or both.

One afternoon, she came home from picking dandelion greens to find him lying in bed, drunk again. He woke up and started mouthing off to her and she lost her cool.

In her words, "I went to my pantry to get my gun. I'd had it with his shit. I didn't mean to play around, I meant to paralyze that bastard once and for all. I went in my bedroom and seen him lyin' on my bed and said, 'Goddamn motherfucker, get ready, this is it!' Then I shot him five times and he bled all over my bed."

Livinia was convicted and got 40 years. The Police Department gave her a medal.

* * * * *

Speaking of getting 40 years at the age of 80, we once had a guy who got 40 years when he was about 65. He looked up at the judge and pleaded, "But judge, I'll never make it that long."

The judge looked down with his soft, brown eyes and in his kindliest voice replied, "That's all right, just do as much of it as you can."

~

The victim complained that the older man reached down the front of his trousers and groped his *gentiles*.

~

HE DONE HER WRONG

Another shooting occurred when Candy B found her pimp, Ronnie C in *flagrante delicto* with Barbara W. They were in a car and took off to leave the scene, but before getting far, got caught behind traffic at a red light.

As they waited for traffic to clear, Candy walked up and commented, "Well, Mr. and Mrs. C, isn't that just precious!"

That said, she pumped one into Ronnie and St. Paul came up short one pimp that night. More's the pity.

~

Found among the defendant's possessions, was a stolen boat *wench*.

Makes you wonder if he had a house wench too.

~

THEY WENT DOWN IN A BLAZE OF GLORY

Over the years, some great arson cases have come across my desk. One involved a husband-wife combination in the suburb of White Bear Lake.

An older man, about 55 and almost stone deaf, married for the first time a 19-year-old girl from rural Minnesota. She was just itching to see the big city and bright lights. Before the honeymoon was even over, her 20-year-old brother moved in with them, also eager to get in on the excitement.

As so often occurs, the big town turned out to be not a whole lot more exciting than the farm — imagine their bitter disappointment. Pa, as we shall come to know him, sanded ski poles for a living at a local ski shop (thereby exceeding his Peter Principle ever so slightly).

The problem seemed to be lack of money, as Pa's meager salary did not lend itself to a good deal of profligate living. The newfound wife and her brother figured if there was just a little more money, they could enjoy the finer cultural advantages city life had to offer (such as a few evenings attending stock car races or demolition derbies).

They convinced Pa that if the house he owned and paid for over the last 25 years, were just to burn down, considerable ready cash could be generated from the insurance proceeds.

At this point occurred some of the most meticulous planning I have ever encountered — things the average person would never think of. For instance, Pa took the precaution of calling his insurance company and, after identifying himself, inquired if his house were to burn down, how much money would they pay him and how long would it take to get the check? Your ordinary arsonist for profit will overlook nice little touches like that.

Then on the evening in question, they took the added precaution of moving all the good furniture from the house to the detached garage, so it wouldn't burn. This wouldn't seem too obvious to investigators later viewing the scene. Actually, a slight oversight in the planning stage occurred here, as they failed to realize the insurance on the house covered the contents as well, but nobody is perfect.

Then they soaked a rug in kerosene and took it in the house, setting it on fire. They shut all the doors and windows and spent the night in a motel. The next morning, they drove by to view the ruin, but as luck would have it, they had closed the house up so tightly, the fire lacked sufficient oxygen and extinguished itself after smoking the place up pretty good.

Being of a persistent nature, they determined to give it another go the next night. On this occasion, the bride and her brother dropped Pa off near the house. As he went up with an empty coke bottle to drain a little more kerosene from a barrel in the garage to pour on the corner of the house, they decided he was getting to be something of a pain in the butt and had to be gotten rid of.

They stopped at a nearby pay phone and called the cops, anonymously informing them of the impending arson at the correct address. Immediately, and before Pa could light the place up, the sirens started blaring. He got spooked, so he started running headlong into nowhere. He ran and ran, aimlessly, all night long. At one point, he swam across a short bay of White Bear Lake and continued running straight to the police station, where he blurted out the whole story.

We generally solve tough cases like this. This one resulted in The Clyde M Award being shared three ways for the first and only time.

* * * * *

Investigators, once again, encountered some of the most fiendishly clever planning ever exhibited by an arsonist. Ronnie and Leon W had gone to a filling station a whole block distant from the scene of the fire and purchased two gallons of gasoline. Because they had no containers, they also purchased two one-gallon "Easy Pour" containers. As they had no money, they left two rings as collateral for their purchase. Hardly anyone would take notice of, or recall such a transaction.

Then, so as not to arouse too much suspicion by buying too much gas at one station, they went across the street to the other station on that corner and bought two more gallons of gas, two more containers to hold the gas and left two more rings.

Investigators at the fire scene found three of the "Easy Pour" containers in the basement and one by the back door. Burn patterns in the basement showed a large quantity of gasoline had been thrown up against the ceiling which then dripped down to the floor. A trail of gas had been poured from the center of the basement and up the back stairs for use as a makeshift fuse. Leon, we later learned, stood at the back door and lit a match.

I'm told that a gallon of gasoline, mixed for optimum performance, is the equivalent of several sticks of dynamite. Cousin Willie's place was absolutely blown to kingdom-come. Only one wall was left standing. The back wall, where Leon was standing, was blown out in one piece and rested against the building behind Cousin Willie's. The destruction was total and instantaneous.

Leon lived to go to trial, but he wished he hadn't — and not just because he was convicted. While he was in the hospital burn unit, he was visited by a friend, who at the time was a police informant. He told her, and she related to the police, his friends were bringing heroin to him in the hospital and there was no amount of heroin he could take to ease the pain.

Every now and then, justice take a kind of poetic form. Leon won the Clyde M Award that year.

A REALLY FOUL MOUTH

Another instance of poetry in justice occurred during one of the gasoline shortages during the early '70's. As usual, we started getting our share of gasoline siphoning.

In one case, a guy owned a large motor home which was fully equipped — it even had toilet and a holding tank. One night, a thief came to siphon some gasoline using the tried and true method of sucking on a rubber hose. In his anxious confusion, and because it was dark, he managed to insert the hose into the toilet holding tank.

A large quantity of vomit was observed trailing away from the scene. Although the thief was not apprehended, it was thought substantial justice had been achieved.

~

At the scene of the burglary, a *bowel* of soup was found on the table.

~

THE SHOOT OUT

One police report, which always amused me, was about two guys who were in a small, 10-by-10 foot bedroom, arguing over who had first dibs on the woman lying on the bed. One word led to another and they each drew — one had a .44 and the other a .38. In all, twelve shots were fired and no one was hit, although they all went deaf. Occasionally, miracles occur.

IF YOU WANT THE JOB DONE RIGHT, DO IT YOURSELF

An interesting case was once solved, in a manner of speaking, during the preparation of a famous murder trial. A prisoner in the jail wanted to see the County Attorney and was escorted to the office. He told us another prisoner was armed with a knife and planned to kill a prisoner who was a key witness in the murder trial. The jail cell was searched, the weapon found and the planned killing averted.

During the course of the conversation, the prisoner seemed anxious to talk about another case involving a theft, which had occurred several years before. In that instance, a large number of wigs were stolen from a warehouse. Its notoriety drew our attention at the time, but nothing ever came of it and the statute of limitations expired.

Our informant told us that the owner of the warehouse had told him that if he could steal a number of wigs, the warehouse owner would make it worth his while. He went on to say that he subcontracted the job to one Rudy E, but neglected to tell Rudy who the prime contractor was. Imagine the chagrin when Rudy, in his ignorance, stole the wigs from the person who was scheduled to buy them. Occasionally crooks suffer mix-ups too.

~

The victim (of rape) was wearing *stir-up* (stirrup) pants.

Was it any wonder?

~

THE PRACTICAL JOKE

One time, two guys went to a party together in a car with others and, during the course of the party, the two got into a fight. After the party was over and they were all going home, the winner made the grave tactical mistake of sitting in the front seat with the loser in the back. The loser took a small knife and held the opened blade between his fingers in such a manner that only about an eighth of an inch was exposed beyond his fingertips. He then drew this across his adversary's throat, who told police, "I felt my throat being cut and saw all this blood on my shirt front, so I looked in the mirror and saw my throat was cut from ear to ear. I thought to myself, Oh, no. I'm going to cash in all my chips."

The guy with the knife told the police, "I was just funning him a little."

SOME UNUSUAL SEX OFFENSES

Several years ago, St. Paul suffered a number of thefts of a highly unusual nature. Large, over-the-road tractors; Kenworths,

Whites, Autocars, Peterbilts — you name it — were being stolen. Inevitably, they were recovered, often close to the scene of the theft, but always under the mysterious circumstance of having been driven carefully, so that the front bumper was up against a concrete abutment, but without damage. Indications pointed to the truck having been put in super-low and the clutch engaged, for the drive wheels dug holes as if they had been spinning.

Finally the solution to this puzzler came about when police encountered one such truck at about 3:00 AM, driven up against a concrete abutment, jumping up and down, in a manner of speaking, with its rear wheels spinning. Inside was a young man who turned out to be a seminary student.

His frame of mind was such that he could not bring himself to commit the sin of masturbation. His method of release was to steal a truck, ease it up against an obstacle, lie down with his exposed penis on the seat, engage the drive and let nature take its course.

* * * * *

Police once responded to a call with one of the most horrendous injuries any man can imagine. The victim's complaint was that two unknown men, whom he could not describe, broke into his apartment on a Saturday morning and attacked him by inserting his penis into the nozzle end of an Electrobroom vacuum sweeper. A neighbor in an adjoining apartment noted the Electrobroom had been running all morning, and had been run for long periods on other occasions. In any case, the victim came up about one-and-a-half inches short when his penis got caught in the impeller.

* * * * *

Exposers, "flashers" as they are known, are among the most recidivistic and unusual culprits in the human lexicon. On one such occasion, I had a conversation with a psychologist who was trying to treat such offenders with aversion therapy a `la *Clockwork Orange*. I asked him how it was going and he told me he was abandoning the technique.

He had gotten a referral from court who had pled guilty to indecent exposure. Almost immediately after the first session, the guy was caught flashing five different women. The doctor, disturbed by this ugly turn of events, went to the jail to visit his patient and inquired what did he think he was doing?

He received the reply, "Well, I thought since you'd probably have me cured soon, I'd better do as much of it as I could while the doing was good."

* * * * *

The flasher who most impressed himself on my attention was one who could only perform under the most rigorous conditions. He invariably would be driving a car and would pull alongside the right side of a bus in motion. Then, if he could catch the eye of some woman in the bus, he would flash her, following along with the bus for several blocks if it didn't have to pull over to pick up or let off fares.

Some day, the bus will pull over when his attention is diverted and he's going to be in a terrible wreck. How'd you like to explain that to the cops?

* * * * *

The most bizarre sex case it has ever been my pleasure to encounter, concerned a local hairdresser a number of years ago. Several women came to the St. Paul Police all with the same complaint. It seems that after he washed and set their hair, he placed them in one of a number of small booths in a back room to sit under the dryer. The front of each booth was covered with some sort of drape that hung right to the floor. Running along in front of the line of booths was a very thick, electrical cord.

As they entered the booth, each woman would be told the electricity was not working correctly and it would be necessary for her to take her shoes off, slip her toes out under the drape and step on and kick the electric cord repeatedly to keep "the juice flowing." The complaint was that after a few minutes, they would wind up with this whitish, sticky fluid all over their feet. Some of these women managed to reach some seemingly far-fetched conclusions as to the source of this fluid.

A policewoman was assigned to investigate this phenomenon. After her hair was washed and cut, she went into the booth and was given the same spiel. Shortly after she started with her foot, she pulled the drape aside to find the hair stylist on the floor with his exposed penis under her foot. It became apparent the complaining witnesses' stories were not so far-fetched after all.

This case came to be known as the "toe job" or the "kick off." Variety is the spice of life, I guess.

* * * * *

The following two cases do not quite fit the category of sex crimes, but have sexual overtones of sorts.

In Minnesota, the County Attorney has the duty of prosecuting paternity cases, in an effort to collect support from the fathers of children born out of wedlock. One such case was being prosecuted in Hennepin County. Just before they entered the courtroom, the mother showed the prosecutor a photo she said her girlfriend had taken, asking if it would help.

The photo depicted her lying nude on a bed, and the nude putative father standing alongside the bed, with a large grin on his face and an erection. The prosecutor said he thought it would.

Unlike a criminal case, the prosecution is permitted, in paternity cases, to call the defendant to the stand and cross-examine him. In this case, the testimony consisted mostly of the defendant denying *any* acquaintanceship with the mother. He was then confronted with the photo. He looked at it for a while, looked up at the judge, examined the picture again, looked at the jury, examined the picture some more and finally said, "That does sorta look like me."

The defense counsel examined the picture, asked for a recess and settled the case.

* * * * *

This next case involved a stock clerk at a 24-hour convenience store, who was suspected of stealing. The management surreptitiously placed a surveillance camera in the store, aimed at the cash register. Sure enough, about midnight, when there were no customers in sight, the culprit sneaked a $20 bill into his pocket and, while the register drawer was open, masturbated onto the remaining money. He, too, wanted a trial until his lawyer viewed the videotape.

BAD CHECKS

Leaving sex offenders, we turn now to frauds. Most confidence men (confidence *persons,* in this age of political correctness) we encounter are pretty small potatoes; penny ante check forgers who, in their own fiendishly clever way, make the checks payable to their own name and then wonder how the police managed to catch them so quickly.

One such person was Howard H, whose only ambition was to go back to prison. Prison was home for him. All his friends were there, his meals were provided, he had a warm bed, television — everything he could want. Howard H couldn't cope with the real world.

One time, the detective in charge of the check division called him in and told him to quit writing his own name in as the payee on these forged checks, he was making it too easy. Sure enough, the next time he got out, he wrote a whole bunch of forged checks — with himself as the payee.

* * * * *

The con man that displayed the greatest flair was Albertus B. He was a large, robust, middle-aged man with a ready smile and firm handshake. He projected an air of causal confidence — the hall mark of a good con man. One bright sunny day in 1968, he walked into a local Cadillac dealership with a woman he called his wife. After kicking the tires on a number of Cadillacs, he called a salesman over to quietly, and very confidentially, tell him, "The woman over there, she's my wife. I just learned today that she has cancer, but she doesn't know it yet. I want to do something special for her before she goes; how much is that Cadillac convertible?"

At the time, it was about $8,000, which would translate into about $40,000 in today's economy. Albertus wrote out a check for the full amount on a small out-of-town bank and said they would be in Monday to pick the car up, thus giving the salesman time to get it serviced and ready.

Monday came and went, and no sign of Albertus. Tuesday he came in, all out of breath and announced, "Sorry I couldn't make it yesterday. The workmen just came to put the new swimming pool in and I had to stay and see it was done right." Albertus drove off with the car, and it turned out he had $28 in his account.

So far, the story is unremarkable — most prosecutors have heard it a thousand times. Albertus' next move showed a certain panache, though, as he parlayed the car into much larger sums.

Albertus and his "wife" drove the car to a popular vacation spot, Alexandria, Minnesota, this being the middle of summer. Just before driving into town, he put the top down and taped some large, full length banners on the sides of the car, proclaiming, "Mrs. America of 1968."

He drove around the town, convincing everyone his wife had just won the Mrs. America of 1968 contest, and was given this brand-new Cadillac convertible and a one week vacation in Alexandria, Minnesota. Everyone was mightily impressed and Albertus drove around town and importuned every merchant up and down the street to cash a sizable check for him, as he just happened to be a little short of cash. Nearly everyone was happy to oblige and before it was all over, he raised nearly $12,000. We in St. Paul had a warrant out for him on the car deal, as did Alexandria for his check passing there. They caught him first and had him in their jail.

The next thing I knew, I was being visited by a preacher who was something of a constant nuisance (always wanting us to raid the penny ante State Fair gambling games, and conduct other worthy projects of that nature). He told a tale of woe that Albertus was now at the University Hospital; the Alexandria Sheriff released him. Long ago, while working during the winter for the State Highway Department, he froze his feet and was probably going to have them amputated. He might not even survive this operation and the charges were so disturbing to his psyche. Couldn't I find it in my heart, as a decent Christian, to release our charge against him?

The short answer was, "No," but it took an hour to say it over and over against the lamentations of the preacher.

In less than a week, the same preacher called to inquire whether the charges had been dropped. Again I said no and he replied, "That's good, because the S.O.B. borrowed my new Buick and $8,000 and is now somewhere in Florida."

The milk of human kindness no longer flowed through the preacher's veins.

*   *   *   *   *

Bad check victims, especially banks, are notoriously lax in taking precautionary measures. They've tightened up their act a little bit, lately, but still need to exercise more caution. Once reason is they hire tellers straight out of high school, give them one half-day's on the job training and trust them to handle thousands of dollars of customer money.

This is best illustrated by the story of a local suburban bank which once canceled a depositor's checking account for constant overdrafts. For four consecutive months thereafter, the depositor cashed about $300 to $400 worth of checks each month at the very bank which closed his account.

*   *   *   *   *

Another case was presented to us where the suspect bought a used car with a check which contained all the information a normal check would, but omitted the name of the bank. There was a real nice picture of a bank, Greco-Roman columns and all, in the upper left hand corner, but no name on the bank where the check could be cashed. It amounted to little more than an IOU.

*   *   *   *   *

One unusual forged check case occurred when a burglar broke in a woman's house and stole her checkbook. Then he promptly went to a nearby restaurant, filled out the check and presented it for cashing. The trouble was, he gave the check to the woman who owned the house he burglarized, and whose name he forged. Usually, we need two witnesses on a check forgery; the person whose name was forged on the check and the person who accepted the forged check. This time we saved witness fees and were able to get away with only one.

* * * * *

In recent years, a number of "Unbanks" or "Cashland" places have opened, specializing in cashing checks for people. They were the target of bad check artists for quite a while, however, they did a pretty good job of screening the checks they took, and most now have remote electronic door devices which enable the clerk to lock suspects in until police arrive. Nonetheless, we have had some "slow learners" who, notwithstanding the fact they have been arrested once, have gone back to the same place within a week to cash another forged check, only to be locked in and arrested again.

* * * * *

Often the person who cashes these checks will have someone's stolen checkbook, and will write out the name printed at the top of the check in the space for the maker. One such crook, a black man with very obvious African American features, did just exactly this, writing out the name Chong Vang in front of the clerk. The clerk was neither fooled nor amused. I wasn't fooled either, but I was amused.

Another winner of the Clyde M Award.

* * * * *

Fenton V operated a large check-cashing ring, and had taken the merchants in town for several tens-of-thousands of dollars. He himself never cashed the checks, but information came to the police he was the brains behind the operation. For several weeks undercover police followed Fenton.

Nearly every night, he left his home to go to the Mt. Airy Bar. There he always met up with two associates, Gerald I and Marlow S. He would meet them in a back booth, sit for a short time and leave. His two associates, Gerald and Marlow, would then leave and go to another bar habituated almost exclusively by alcoholic down-and-outers. Each would recruit about three or four of these inebriated souls and take them to local Target Stores, supermarkets and the like. Each would be given about three checks from some corporation and ID which matched their general description.

The check cashers would go into the store, cash the check and return to Gerald and Marlow. The guys cashing the checks were given about $25 for each check cashed and returned to their bar, where they continued to poison themselves. Gerald and Marlow would then return to the Mt. Airy Bar, about 10:00 PM to meet with Fenton. After a short time, they would all leave again.

In order to get a search warrant together, police tailed all three of these guys through several complete operations of the type described above. A search warrant was then obtained for Fenton's home. Inside, was one room devoted entirely to checkbooks stolen from businesses. Also found was a suitcase full of driver's licenses and other similar ID, stolen during various strong-arm robberies. There were enough of these to match almost anybody's description. A check protector and typewriter were also found, and the printing and type from these matched that placed on all the checks in question.

Because this was such a large and profitable operation, I requested a high bail. Fenton protested and claimed he was a long term resident of St. Paul, and gave the address where the search warrant was executed as his permanent home. This worked greatly to his detriment when at the trial, after being confronted with all the damning evidence, he denied this was his home address. We were allowed to impeach this testimony with his former claims made at the bail hearing.

The total cost of the undercover operation was very high because of the enormous amount of manpower involved. For instance, one could not use the same people over and over again, as they would be spotted. The same was true of cars.

The cost to Fenton was 10 years.

SNITCHES

Police, in their efforts to solve tough crimes will, of necessity, talk to people in the criminal world. This is their best source of information. Such people tend to become very talkative when in jail facing heavy time. They'll promise all kinds of marvelous results if the cop can just get them back on the street for a couple of days. These things seldom pay off, but sometimes result in bizarre happenings.

One such occasion occurred when Walter R was in jail for a robbery. He told an officer he could solve a particularly nettlesome murder if he could just get out for a couple of days. The officer, convinced this guy could help, came to me and I went to a judge and got the defendant's bail lowered to nearly nothing.

That night, our informant got drunk with a famous alcoholic named "Kreepy K The Child Molester," or so the tattoo on his shoulder read. The next morning the detective came into my office and explained, "Walter R just killed a guy last night."

"What!!!" I came out of my seat, "What are you talking about?"

"They were playing Russian Roulette," replied the detective.

According to the two girlfriends who were there, they were sitting across from each other at a long dining table and Kreepy pulled out a revolver and said, "You know what I think I'm gonna do? I think I'm gonna shoot you in the head." He fired and purposely missed, saying, "Ah, gee. I missed. Why don't you shoot me?"

Kreepy then handed the gun to Walter, who repeated the process, missed and gave the gun back to Kreepy. This went back and forth several times, and each time was accompanied by a big swig on the whiskey bottle. Eventually, Walter, in his drunken stupor, managed to shoot Kreepy right between the running lights. Investigators found several slugs in the two walls at each end of the room, indicating the women were probably telling the truth.

So much for snitches.

*   *   *   *   *

There was in St. Paul, a snitch so famous, his nickname came to be "Snitchin' Bill S." Snitchin' Bill was in the dope business and he would try to eliminate his competition by putting the police on them. Occasionally, the police would raid Snitchin' Bill's place and he, too, would have to do a little time.

Once, they raided him in the winter when the snow was about three feet deep on the ground. His place was sufficiently well barricaded so it took a little while to bust in. When they did, there was no Bill and no dope. As they searched through the place, they found Bill had fashioned a tunnel from boards and cardboard, leading from his basement window, through the snow, out to his garage, enabling him to get out with his stash before the police got in.

One night, two Captains of the respective Homicide Divisions of St. Paul and Minneapolis, were out drinking and the subject of Snitchin' Bill came up. After the bars closed, the Captain from Minneapolis claimed to be very close to Bill and suggested to the St. Paul Captain they go over to his house for a drink.

"You'll never get in there," replied the St. Paul Captain. The Minneapolis Captain insisted Bill would let them in. They bet $100 on it and each took off in their separate cars. In route, the St. Paul Captain called a friend at the station and told him to call Snitchin' Bill and inform him they were on the way to raid his joint.

St. Paul won the bet.

*   *   *   *   *

Another famous snitch was Elmer C. He ran a tippling house where, as it was put, *other unscheduled social activities* occurred. He was the favorite snitch of the Captain in charge of the Robbery Division. One time a drunk staggered out of Elmer's and was set upon by two young thugs, who beat him up and robbed him. The victim was so drunk at the time, police knew he would never be able to prove a case against anyone. The Robbery Division Captain called Elmer and told him this would be bad for business; the cops were going to have to start watching his place closer. Elmer assured him this problem would be taken care of.

A couple days later, the Captain noticed a report on two young toughs, who were in the hospital suffering from being severely pistol whipped. They claimed not to know who attacked them. As he read the report, the phone rang. When he answered it, the only thing said on the other end was, "The deed is did, baby," and the line went dead.

Sad to say, Elmer died in a shoot-out, during which he and his attacker both loudly alluded to the seriousness of the other's Oedipus complex. Elmer's downfall was, he always loaded a blank as the first round of his revolver.

On one occasion, he saved a cop who was being attacked by firing in the air, thus scaring off the attacker. As Captain Barkley said, "Elmer was a humanitarian." He was sadly missed by the entire police department. His last X-rays revealed wounds from about four other shoot-outs.

IT WAS A BAD DAY

The same cop who was involved with Walter R and Kreepy K had a sort of penchant for getting into funny situations. On one such occasion he was put in contact, while working on an undercover detail, with a woman who wanted to hire him to kill her husband. They discussed the plan and she wanted him to do the job for $50. My cop friend explained this was a little cheap for such a job.

In order to prosecute a such a case, which would be a conspiracy, we needed something more than "mere talk." We needed an overt act. The cop was told to make her take him to where her husband worked and point him out, which would be enough to constitute an overt act. They did this, and the cop was wired with a small portable microphone. When he wanted her arrested, he was to give the signal, which consisted of him saying, "It's a horseshit day."

His fellow officers decided to play a joke on him and ignore the agreed-on signal. He must have said, "It's a horseshit day," about two dozen times before he finally just gave up and arrested the woman himself.

THE GREAT FUR HEIST

The next case was one from Minneapolis, in which a reported opinion of the Minnesota Supreme Court is on file, and so I feel no compunction to disguise names. The name of the case is *State v. McGlynn*, reported at 195 N.W., page 584, and I quote directly from the opinion.

"Defendant was the mastermind of a blundered fur robbery on December 12, 1968. At about noon of that day, defendant borrowed a blue, 1963 Oldsmobile from Herbert Wroge, a used car salesman, on the pretense of taking it to his wife for approval. The automobile was later identified by others as the get-away vehicle. At about 2:30 PM, defendant and Raymond Stanley Smith (an accomplice who did not testify as state's witness) approached Antell, who was walking with his girl friend, Gail Dubak, and asked whether he "wanted to go on a score." Although Antell initially refused, he reconsidered after defendant assured him that the 'score was real easy.' Mrs. Dubak did not hear the conversation since, at Antell's suggestion, she had continued walking to a nearby store to wait for him. Shortly thereafter, Antell and Mrs. Dubak accompanied defendant and Smith to Mary Anderson's apartment, which Smith shared with Mrs. Anderson, a divorcee. The presence of these persons together at the apartment both before and after the robbery was, as hereafter noted, attested by other witnesses.

"At the apartment, Antell, at defendant's direction, shaved off his beard and mustache and put on dress clothes supplied by defendant. Defendant gave Mrs. Anderson a blond wig to wear in the robbery, a wig similar to that which defendant gave for safekeeping to his downstairs neighbor, Colleen Clark, a few days after the robbery. Defendant, at the same time, handed a loaded .22-caliber revolver to Antell and supplied Antell and Smith with nylon hosiery with which to bind the persons to be robbed, and laundry bags to carry the stolen furs.

"Smith, Antell and Mrs. Anderson then proceeded to execute the robbery of the Gershkow Fur Company at 1013 West Broadway, Minneapolis. Smith and Mrs. Anderson, who had previously visited the Gerskow store, pretending to look at furs, entered first. As Mrs.

Anderson was trying on a fur jacket, Antell entered twirling the revolver on his finger and at some point he shot his own finger, an injury later observed by others. After tying up Gershkow and his wife with the nylon hosiery, Antell and Smith filled the laundry bags with furs, but they had tied up Gerskow so ineffectively that he immediately escaped after they had left the store. Gershkow observed the blue Oldsmobile get-away car and ran to it, grabbing the car door handle. This so startled the robbers that they rear-ended another automobile. They drove away, but Gershkow noted the license number and reported it to the police.

"The errant trio returned to the Anderson apartment. Antell proceeded to place the laundry bag loaded with stolen furs into a panel truck which defendant had stated would be parked there for that purpose. However, the truck proved to be an exterminator's van, and Smith ran back from the apartment to assist Antell in carrying the loot into the apartment.

"Defendant came to the apartment later to pick up the furs. Mrs. Dubak and Kathleen LaFore, a baby sitter for Mrs. Anderson's children, observed defendant moving laundry bags in the apartment, and Mrs. Dubak saw defendant leave the premises carrying two large white bags which 'looked like they were full of something.' These bags were like those defendant supplied to Antell and Smith prior to the robbery. Antell did not deliver all of the stolen furs to defendant but hid one fur coat under the bed before defendant came. He later offered to sell the coat to one Tim Janzen who, having read of the Gershkow fur robbery, turned the fur coat over to the police. Defendant himself sold one of the furs to his neighbor, Colleen Clark, who likewise turned the coat over to the police. Mrs. Gershkow subsequently identified one of the fur coats for the police from hand embroidery she had done on the inside of the coat."

On these facts, defendant's conviction was upheld at the appellate level. Occasionally, Minneapolis criminals prove to be nearly the equal of St. Paul's for ineptitude.

NO QUESTIONS ASKED

One night, two off duty St. Paul Police were sitting in an East-Side bar when "Red" came busting through the back door and asked, "Does anyone wanna buy a hot outboard motor?" The cops acted interested and Red took them out back and showed it to them, still hanging on the transom of a boat he trailed behind his car.

"Is it really hot?" asked one of the cops, ingenuously.

"Of course it's hot," replied Red: "I don't sell nothin' that ain't hot, but don't worry about it, because I stole it way up north and it will never be traced down here."

The two cops said they'd buy, but needed about an hour to get the cash together. Red agreed to meet them at his place. The cops alerted uniform officers who were close at hand when the transaction occurred. Red was arrested and he and the motor were hauled off.

One patrol cop, at the edge of what was going on, was leaving after he heard the arrest was completed. He drove down an alley and saw a garage door open, the light was on and a guy was standing inside, almost salivating on an outboard motor. The cop stopped and walked up to the door and as soon as the guy saw him, he stuck his hands straight up in the air and said, "You got me."

"What do you mean," asked the cop.

"I just bought this motor from Red," replied the citizen.

"Is it stolen?" asked the cop.

"Of course it's stolen," replied the citizen. "Red don't sell nuthin' that ain't stolen."

He and his motor were also taken into custody.

This occurred on a Friday night. The cops could not find where this motor was stolen from (they did find a report of a stolen motor on the one they got from Red). A detective interviewed Red on Monday morning and was told, "You know, the motor I sold that guy down the alley wasn't really stolen — it was mine. I told him it was, and was going to report it stolen to my insurance company, but the fact is, it's the first time I ever sold a motor that wasn't stolen."

It cost the guy a lost weekend for his trouble.

*   *   *   *   *

A young woman was found dead in Como Park. She had last been seen in the company of a suspect and, following my advice, they went to interview him in his home in the presence of his parents — no Miranda warning.

They started out telling him they were investigating the death of this woman and commented he had been the last one seen with her. He was told he was not under arrest and asked what light he might shed on the situation. He immediately started crying and went to his room. The two detectives played it cool and sat, having a cup of coffee with his parents. They young man came out and before he could say anything, he started crying again. The detectives then said they were leaving, but left their card in case he wanted to call them.

They went out to their car, but instead of leaving, they sat and watched the house. After about five minutes, the suspect came running out to the car, got in the back seat, crying all the while, and said, "I did it. I'm the one who killed her." With that they arrested him and were driving him back to St. Paul.

He then said, "That's not the only one you're looking at me for is it?" The officers assured him it was the only one. He said, "No you're looking at me for that other one, too." They only said no, this is the only one. Before he got to the station, he confessed to another murder, without a single question being asked.

* * * * *

A somewhat similar case of willing confession occurred when a robber came into a bar and held it up. He wound up shooting and killing a customer. A police artist made a sketch from descriptions given by the patrons, most of whom were drunk.

A new detective in the Homicide Division was looking through unsolved cases and came across a sketch. He commented to the captain it looked like a very distant relative of his. The captain commented, unless they got a confession, it probably wouldn't go very far because all the victims had been so drunk.

The detective then saw the suspect at a family reunion, walked up and told him, privately, they were looking at him for that killing and one these days they would be coming for him. This happened several more times over the years and, finally, one day he walked into the station and confessed the robbery and murder to the desk sergeant.

His defense counsel approached me and said, "I think this guy is crazy. He's convinced the FBI has been on his tail ever since this happened."

DON'T QUIT THE DAY JOB

Going back to the Clyde M Award for a minute, his cousin, Vernon M almost retired the award one year, with two notable escapades.

In the first case, Vernon burglarized a house and stole mostly jewelry. He previously stole a car for use as a getaway vehicle, but because it was winter and the car he stole was an old beater, it wouldn't start. Vernon noted during his efforts to restart the car, that the owner of the house he just burglarized returned home. Vernon returned to the scene of the crime to borrow some jumper cables. The owner, aware by then he had been burglarized, noted some of his jewelry hanging out of Vernon's pocket and called the police.

A few weeks later, while out on bail, Vernon burglarized what we have come to know as a "garbage house." Every now and then, owners of old, derelict houses abandon them and, in a short time, the place fills up with the garbage and junk of everybody in the area. On this occasion, Vernon went in and purloined a large, heavy, non-working piece of television equipment which had a high negative retail value.

~

The doctor drew a *vile* of blood from the suspect.

He was a pretty vile suspect all right.

~

WHO NEEDS CASINOS?

Some of our criminals actually show some imagination and inventiveness. If they would only put their talents to some socially useful purpose, they might actually make a decent living. Parking meter thieves fall into this category.

One guy, in order to save money, would chew a large wad of bubble gum on the way to work each morning. Then when he found an open meter, he would park, stuff the bubble gum wad down the coin slot and push a quarter in behind it. This would usually cause the meter to jam up and not run any time off. It would only cost the city about $250 to repair it.

The other guy could only work on those days in the winter when it became extremely cold. In St. Paul, we get some 20-degree-below-zero days in January and February. These were ideal from this guy's point of view. Armed with a teakettle full of water, he would go around pouring water into the coin slots, stand back and wait for it to freeze and break the meter. Then he would pick up a frozen lump of ice, full of nickels, dimes and quarters and wait for the next meter to crack.

INFAMOUS LAST WORDS

One criminal who met a bad end was Salty Dog M. One night, he made the grave tactical error of turning out the lights and grabbing all the money off the pool table, where a large number of people were shooting dice. About two nights later, one Jessie who lost about $240 as a result of this transaction, came up and put a .38 to Salty's temple and said, "Where's my money?"

Salty's last two words were, "What money?"

*   *   *   *   *

Occasionally, a guy gets it who probably doesn't have it coming. One such case occurred when our victim was visiting a friend who lived on the 5th floor of an apartment house. An urgent knocking came at the door, and the resident explained it might be the police with a search warrant, as he was a crack cocaine dealer. It turned out to be a couple of customers.

The occupant explained to his visiting friend they had better leave out the "back way." To do this, one went out on the balcony and grabbed the railing and climbed over, easing down to the bottom of the iron bars. One then swung in and out a couple of times and on an in-swing, let go and landed on the balcony below. This process was repeated until reaching the ground floor.

Unfortunately, our visitor had not had time to perfect this skill, and in fact made the mistake of trying to swing himself back and forth while still holding on to the top of the railing.

His last two words were, "Oh shiiiiit."

~

Tattoo on the arm of a criminal: Born *too loose*.

~

TIMING IS EVERYTHING

Another improvement to the human gene pool occurred one day when two guys were walking along and found a passing railroad train blocking their path. One of them said, "No problem. All you do is lie down next to the rails and when you hear that first set of clickety-clacks you roll your body into the center between the rails. Wait for the next set of clickety-clacks and roll out on the other side. I'll go first, and show you how — you follow."

So the first guy, the one who was experienced at this procedure, rolled under the train, then out the other side. The one being initiated did the same thing and it worked. He was so impressed, he thought it would be fun to go back again, so they did and it worked again.

"Damn," one of them said. "Now we're on the wrong side again. Oh well, we can just repeat the process and go back again."

They failed to notice the train was picking up speed. The first guy made it okay, and the second guy made it between the rails, but when he went to roll out the other side, the train got him right at the waistline and cut him in half. He was pretty well anesthetized at the time so, hopefully, didn't feel it.

Another winner of the Clyde M Award, posthumously.

~

The victim (of rape) was *chaste* clear across the parking lot.

~

AT LEAST IT DIDN'T HIT THE FAN

Once we had a very serious shooting at a house occupied by a husband and wife team of dope dealers. A disgruntled customer wished to register a complaint. It was feared they would both die, but thanks to the efforts of our fine doctors at St. Paul Ramsey Medical Center, their lives were spared to deal again. Back at the scene, the police roped off the house and grounds with the yellow tape while investigators examined the premises and gathered evidence.

During this time, a guy who was acquainted with the couple, but unaware of what was going on, came along and snuck under the yellow tape and made it into the house. He was met at the back door by a cop who demanded the answers to all kinds of questions.

"Officer," the guy said with insistence. "You gotta let me use the bathroom. I got the runs real bad."

"Yeah, yeah, we've heard that before," replied the cop. "Up against the wall."

"But officer, you don't understand. We're going to have a terrible accident if I don't use the bathroom."

"Up against the wall," the officer said. "We're going to search you."

They had a terrible accident. The cops sent the guy home without searching him.

OUCH THAT HURTS

Police who have dogs often encounter oddball experiences. One even had a quaint way of writing about his dog. One time, a suspect erred by running from the dog and, when he was caught, struggled and attempted to fight the dog. The officer caught up and wrote this of the scene he encountered. "My K-9 partner had attached himself orally to the suspect's groin area and was continuously adjusting his grip."

Sorta brings tears to the eye, doesn't it?

I BEEN WORKIN' ON THE RAILROAD

Willie N was a poor soul who had been done bad wrong. He'd been working for the railroad for 19 years when he took up with a cute young thing and started living with her. Out of love and trust, he gave her his credit card, which she took full advantage of (if I may use a preposition to end a sentence with). Unable to pay for her profligacy, he got a couple of garnishments on his check which, in those days, got you promptly fired. Thus, with only a few months before he could retire, Willie found himself out of a job.

At this point he went just a little crazy. He called his girlfriend and asked her to come over to prepare him a meal, which she did. As he sat there, brooding over the cruel hand fate had dealt him, he suddenly lost it, picked up a knife and stabbed his beloved.

She wasn't hurt too bad and called the police. In jail, as Willie was awaiting trial, his mental condition deteriorated. All night long he would pound on his steel bunk bedsprings like a bongo drum and chant, "Pray for the departed soul of Willie N."

This proved to be terribly disturbing to the other inmates, but not as disturbing as the fact that, on occasion, he would light his mattress on fire as he lay on it, continuing to chant his mournful call, "Pray for the departed soul of Willie N."

The inmates, fearing fire in a jail more than almost anything, would immediately start hollering, "Willie N has set himself on fire again!" The guards would have to come and put him out. I guess in 34 years I never felt so sorry for anyone as I did for Willie.

Willie was convicted of a felony assault but because the judge felt sorry for him, too, he received a very short workhouse term and probation. Often, someone like Willie can make good use of probation services, find a job and stay out of trouble.

~

Upon arresting the defendant, I advised him of his *tights*.

~

JOSE F MISSED HIS CALLING

A shooting of some interest occurred in Jose F's combined gambling-tippling-whorehouse (Jose was a competitor of Marion M). Sherrie F, a professional dancer who was a habitué of Jose's joint, brought a newfound boyfriend in one evening. Sherrie was fetching, as usual, with her dyed purple hair.

Her old flame, John B, just happened to be there by chance. He took some exception to Sherrie's new love interest, and expressed himself to that effect. One word led to another and, pretty soon, John found himself dying on the floor. One slug entered his upper chest and deflected downward off his collar bone and into his liver. One slug hit him in the heart, and the third one got him in the end of the penis (a difficult target to miss, in his case).

Jose F gave the most dramatic testimony in the case. He could not say anything without simultaneously acting it out for the grand jury. He told them as John lay dying on the floor, Sherri came and gave him his good-bye kiss and took his diamond rings (all four) commenting as she did so, "John always told me if anything ever happened to him, he wanted me to have his rings."

As Jose related this, he got down on his knees and demonstrated Sherrie's actions — kissing, removing, etc. Then, so as to be evenhanded in the manner, he also reenacted John's position — flat on his back, getting his good-bye kiss.

"After that," Jose related, "another old girlfriend, Edgreen K, came and gave John a good-bye kiss, and took his wallet, with about $800 in it, from his pocket." Jose reenacted the kissing scene, once again from the point of view of both participants.

John must have died happy, under the circumstances.

TAX EVASION

One day the St. Paul Police saw a drunk staggering down University Avenue with a pair of tin snips in his hand. Aroused by these unusual circumstances, they stopped him to inquire and found the portion of someone's license plate containing the 3-M, annual renewal, sticker-tag for the current year in the drunk's pocket. When they inquired what he was going to do with it, he told them he was going to take it home, boil the sticker off and glue it to his own license plate so he could start driving again.

NO GO

Another winner of the Clyde M award was a young man who went to a party in the nearby suburb of Roseville with some friends, who later ditched him there. Needing a ride home, he broke into a transmission repair shop where there were about six cars all with their transmissions out. Unaware of the exact nature of his surroundings, he started all six cars in an effort to get away, but was unable to get any of them to move. Neighbors heard the racing motors and called the cops, who came and found him still trying to get a car in gear.

LEFT-TURN WILLIE

Speaking of auto thefts reminds me of Willie F He was another who regarded prison as home, but never wanted to do anything too serious. His favorite way of getting caught was to steal a car and drive down University Avenue — a six lane street. Then, when he saw a police car, he would make a left turn from the far right lane, a sure-fire way to get caught.

Willie always wanted to plead guilty, but he always wanted some kind of "deal." At the time, auto theft was a three year offense, and Willie always wanted his sentence to be limited to two-and-a-half years. We usually gave him this concession, and once I asked his lawyer why he wanted a deal when he went to so much trouble to get caught. I was told the prison inmates gave him a hard time if he pled guilty straight up with no deal. Willie would have been happy if auto theft carried a life sentence.

HARI KARI

Police were summoned to a house in St. Paul, where a young man had suffered the very serious injury of being stabbed in the belly. He guts were literally hanging out to his knees. When asked what happened, he related he had been on a bus on University Avenue when, for no reason, some stranger walked up and stabbed him. He said he then left the bus without notifying the driver and made his way to the house where police found him.

This sounded a little fishy and, in fact, the same two cops who answered this call were then dispatched to another house about two blocks away. There, it seems a group of friends were gathered at a woman's house, preparing to go to a party. The lady resident wanted to take a shower before she went, but because there was one person she did not trust, who turned out to be our above mentioned injured party, she took her billfold with her in the bathroom. Her apprehension was justified, because as she showered, he snuck in the bathroom and stole the billfold. She sounded the alarm and others present caught up with the culprit as he tried to leave through the rear door in the kitchen.

They told police their version of what happened. It went something like this: After they confronted him with the stolen wallet, he grabbed a butcher knife from a drawer and started flailing away wildly at them. As he did so, he managed to stab himself, awkwardly, in the belly.

A detective then went to interview him in the hospital and confronted him with this story. He was asked to relate his version of what happened. At this point, he said he would tell the detective what happened to him, but he did not wish to talk about anything that led up to the stabbing. The detective did not interview him further, but came to me for advice. I told him to start working on the next case.

~

The suspect decided to *flea* the scene.

I wondered if he was going to louse it too.

~

THE BEST LAID PLANS...

At about 2:00 AM one morning, police on routine patrol noticed a speeding car. They took off after it and activated their lights and siren. After about 2 blocks, the suspect slammed on the brakes and bailed out. The cops chased him on foot for a distance, but eventually he outran them. Shortly after, they received a call from the resident of a nearby house.

Upon arrival, the lady of the house explained that shortly before, some guy had pushed his way in, brushed her off to one side and ran upstairs. Once there, he ran into a bedroom where another guy was sleeping, stripped off his clothes and jumped in bed with the sleeper. He then pretended to fall asleep, snoring loudly. The cops entered the bedroom only to find the driver of the car, who had outrun them, indignant at their intrusion as he pretended to wake up. All this happened on a Friday night, and the guy spent the entire weekend in jail. Had he just waited and taken his speeding ticket, he would have been turned loose on the spot. Some improvised plans just don't work out too well.

*   *   *   *   *

A young, unsophisticated, 18-year-old girl, the sheltered daughter of a minister, rented a Karaoke machine and had it in the back of her van. Someone broke in and stole it. Unaware her insurance would probably pay for it, she hit upon a weird scheme to raise the enormous sum of $11,000. The scheme was nearly unparalleled in both its complexity and stupidity. She enlisted her roommate, another naïve 18-year-old. Giving the roommate her credit card, she instructed the accomplice to take the credit card and go buy several expensive items, such as diamond rings. Then, she was going to take them back for a refund, and when the credit card bill came, she was going to claim her credit card had been stolen.

These two realized that sometimes, when large purchases are made, clerks ask questions which pertain to personal data relating to the cardholder — such as your mother's maiden name. To cover this, they were going to pretend the girl using the card was from Germany and spoke no English. The girl, whose card it was, would go along and pretend to be the *German* girl's interpreter in order to answer these questions. The girl supposedly from Germany, wore a large babushka and dark-colored glasses in an effort to disguise herself.

Unfortunately, they were such inept actresses, they were unable to carry it off and were caught almost immediately.

~

I questioned the suspect as he *lied* on the ground.

He probably would have lied standing up, too.

~

JUST WHEN YOU THINK THERE ARE NO SURPRISES LEFT

An armed robbery occurred at a suburban drugstore and the culprit got away with quite of bit of cash. The sheriff's patrol responded and Charlie Zacharias, who was later elected sheriff, answered the call. Because it was snowing heavily, he was able to track the getaway car to a point where it had slid off into the ditch. Footprints led away from it, across a field of freshly-fallen snow, to a house. The occupants, a couple of teenagers, let him in and allowed him to search the place. In the bathroom, seated on the throne, was the suspect. A mask and a sack of money were beside him in the wastebasket.

As Charlie interviewed the two teenagers, who were cooperating and telling him about their acquaintance, who had come into the house and ran into the bathroom, another deputy arrived. Since the gun had not been found, Charlie dispatched him to find it. The deputy went through the access hole into the area between the ceiling and the roof and started poking around through the insulation. Suddenly, as Charlie sat at the kitchen table interviewing the witnesses, he heard a terrible crash. Without looking, he knew what happened.

He went into the living room to find the deputy had crashed through the plasterboard in the ceiling. His brown trouser leg with yellow strip, was dangling down from the ceiling and insulation was raining down into the living room.

After he helped his friend out, Charlie drove downtown and wrote the report. The next day he delivered it to me so we could start preparing for the lawsuit which, for some unfathomable reason, never came.

~

Burglary report forms have several boxes to fill out, one of which asks, "How was entry gained?" One answer was, *"Threw* a garage door.*"*

~

SOMETHING WAS LOST IN THE TRANSLATION

M H was a bank robber who encountered a difficult situation one day. There is a large Hmong community in St. Paul, which settled here after the Vietnamese conflict. Our culprit decided to rob a Hmong credit union. He took the precaution of calling ahead of time and inquired whether they spoke English.

"Oh yes, we speak very good English here," came the heavily accented reply.

M H then crafted a note written on both sides, so one could read it no matter which side was up. He took it in, together with a small satchel, which the note explained contained a bomb.

He gave the note to the teller and conspicuously displayed the satchel, all the while demanding money. The teller, a young Hmong male, carefully explained in his pidgin English that they could give money only to Hmong people who were members of the credit union.

The robber protested that this was a robbery, and it didn't matter whether he was Hmong or not because you didn't have to be Hmong to rob the place. The teller continued to explain politely that their charter forbade them to do business with anyone but Hmong people and he could not give the guy any money.

As the robber became more insistent and demanding, the teller called out to a fellow worker in the bank, explaining in Hmong, they were being robbed and to call the police. At this point, the robber commanded the teller not to speak Hmong in his presence, but instead, to speak English only. With that, the teller called out once again to his companion in clear English, "Call the cops, we're being robbed."

The robber was so unnerved, he picked up his note and left.

He was caught several days later, when an FBI snitch, named Leon, turned him in. The snitch was a very muscular person and the FBI promised him a $5,000 reward to help them catch the guy. The snitch arranged for the robber to come to his house then alerted FBI agents. When they closed in on the culprit, they ordered him out and, as he exited, they ordered him to lie down on the ground.

"I can't," he replied, "both my arms are broken."

"How did that happen?" they asked.

"I was visiting this guy, Leon, who broke both my arms and robbed me," he complained.

The snitch collected his reward in advance, and then some.

~

The suspect was so drunk he could *bearly* walk.

~

ME THINKS SHE DOTH PROTEST TOO MUCH

A case was presented in which a Hmong Lady, married, complained to police that a Hmong man, married to a different woman, had raped her approximately 30 times. It always happened the same way. He would wait until her husband went to work and then drive up and honk his horn. She would then go out and get in the car and he would drive off to the most romantic spot he could think of — usually the parking lot at the Montgomery Ward store. There he would rape her and then return her to her home.

For some inexplicable reason, the cad had the unmitigated gall to write her a love letter which contained such memorable phrases as, "My is in think you all time," etc. To compound his error, he placed the note under the windshield wiper of her husband's car. The husband, upon making this startling discovery, confronted his wife, who had to acknowledge she had been raped 30 times over the last three years by this guy. At the husband's insistence, she reported it to the police.

The case didn't go very far.

SAY CHEESE

A number of years ago, the City Attorney who prosecuted misdemeanors in Ramsey County, decided to go on a crusade against pornographic literature. There followed periodic raids on the Carlson Book Store, which carried a large line of such literature along with various related accessories. One time, an Assistant City Attorney named Dan went along. He noted a number of dildos hanging from a string in the window and, wishing to preserve this scene for evidence, turned to the camera cop and said, "Before you leave, take a picture of those pricks in the window."

The cop didn't quite understand what was being asked of him so for his final photo, he lined the four store employees up in front of the window and took their picture.

Imagine Dan's surprise when he got copies of the photos.

SORRY, WRONG NUMBER

St. Paul police solved one homicide in a very unusual way. The murderer felt the need to tell his friend about it so he called him on the phone. Since no one was home, the answering machine came on and the culprit gave a detailed account of the matter on the recorder. He initiated the conversation by saying, "This is Francis P" He told how he stabbed the victim for playing music too loud and stuffed the body in the refrigerator, along with other detailed information about the crime.

Imagine his chagrin when it developed he had dialed the wrong number and was talking to the answering machine of a total stranger, who called the cops.

Another winner of the Clyde M Award.

SHAKEDOWN, RATTLE AND ROLL

Another case of poetic justice occurred when a couple of young toughs stopped a car one hot summer night, in which two guys and their girlfriends were driving along minding their own business.

The man in the back seat got out and was immediately set upon by one of the thugs. The other tough went after the man in the driver's seat, who still had the two girls in his car. He took off and the ruffian grabbed hold of the center post where the two doors come together, as the windows were all rolled down.

The guy hanging onto the car had a knife and was reaching in with his left hand, trying to slash the driver, who kept moving over toward the center of his car. In doing so, he neglected his steering and sideswiped a parked car on the side where his assailant was clinging. As he did so, the body of the attacker was rolled between the two cars, more-or-less as you would roll a pencil between the palms of your hands. He was dead before he hit the ground and his body had cushioned the sides of the two cars so almost no damage was sustained by either of them.

WHAT A LOAD OF GARBAGE

Two guys who were renovating an old house rented a dumpster from *Dick's Dumpsters*. When it was full, Dick came to pick it up and collect his rent money, but they refused to pay. He retaliated by saying, "Okay, then the dumpster sits on your lawn until my bill is paid."

One of the two guys then tried to sell the dumpster. The cops got word of it and inquired what was going on. They told him some guy had abandoned a dumpster full of garbage on their lawn and they were trying to figure out a way to get rid of it. The cop, being a good-natured soul, said, "That's easy. I'll just have the city tow truck take it to the impound lot."

The next person he heard from was Dick, who wanted to know what was going on. This, of course, was after a $300 towing and storage bill had been accumulated. Dick also got to pay the bill and was told to sue the owners of the house, who had ordered the dumpster out.

~

In the men's room we found two *dinks* sitting on the urinal.

~

DOWN BUT NOT OUT

One time a woman, Lavonne M, went out and found a drunk in a bar and took him home to have some coffee. As he sat in the living room, she and her other male companion sent her 5-year-old daughter in to sit on the guy's lap. Then they rushed in and accused the guy of molesting the daughter. She started whipping him with a doubled up cord from an electric iron.

Pretty soon, her other male companion said, "Wait a minute, Lavonne, maybe we can settle the civil liability here." He turned to the guy and said, "Do you have any money?" At this point, the drunk showed the greatest presence of mind he ever had in his entire lifetime. "Yes, but it's in the bank."

They waited until morning and took him to the First National Bank in St. Paul. The guy knew a guard would be there. The minute he saw him, he ran up to him and said, "Arrest these two, they are trying to rob me!"

They both did some pretty heavy time for that. Naturally, the guy didn't have a cent in the bank.

A CRAZY SCHEME

A poor soul deposited his check in his bank and was met, immediately after, by a stranger who asked if he had an account at that bank. "Yes. Why do you ask?"

"Well," said the stranger, "I tried to cash a check here and they wouldn't take it because I don't have an account here, but they said if someone with an account would endorse it, they would take it. If you'll do this for me, I'll give you $20."

The account holder thought that was a terrific deal, and endorsed the $400 check and got his $20. The other guy said, "I'm a stranger here in town, and I wonder if you could show me around."

"Sure," said the victim. They went to Minneapolis and hit all the bars, the stranger in town even bought a suit. Then he said he'd run out of money and if they could go cash another check, he'd give the same deal — $20 for the endorsement. The account holder agreed.

After cashing the second check, they parted ways, but before the account holder left the bank, a teller told him she didn't think the checks were any good, for a number of reasons.

"Why did you take them?" asked the account holder. It was then he learned, for the first time, that if they bounced, the money would be withdrawn from his account for having endorsed the checks.

We caught the culprit later, who turned out to be an escapee from an Illinois mental institution.

THE BAD TRIP

A lady cop with a police dog, Cato, was driving down the street and saw two teenagers in a yard. As she drove by, one of them broke a window in the house and crawled in, right before her eyes. She and Cato got out and she asked the one outside what was going on. He told her his friend was having a bad LSD trip and acting crazy. About this time, the homeowner came running out, complaining of the break-in.

The cop and her dog entered the house and demanded the suspect surrender. When he failed to do so, she turned Cato loose. He ran to the kitchen in the back and started biting the suspect, who fought back and actually succeeded in getting the dog off of him. The cop came in to assist the dog and pretty soon, she, the suspect and the dog were are crashing through the kitchen, rolling around on the floor in one big fat melee, knocking over the table and chairs and breaking them all up.

Meanwhile, the homeowner and the suspect's friend called paramedics, who arrived in the middle of the fight. They entered the house and because Cato was having so little luck subduing the suspect, he took out after them and started biting. Finally the suspect was subdued and taken in. The house was a shambles.

The next day the suspect explained he had a bad LSD trip and thought he was dead. He saw a lady cop and thought she was taking him to hell. He then decided if he could get in the house, he could avoid her, but the next thing he knew, he was fighting with a dog from hell.

Let that be a lesson to you if you're inclined toward LSD.

TOO BAD THE CLYDE M AWARD WAS ONLY FOR THE CRIMINALS

One time, a guy who was in the business of selling what has come to be known as "turkey" (a slang for fake dope), made arrangements to sell about $3,000 worth to an undercover cop. In this case however, the dope dealer had no intention of selling even turkey. He was going to flat-out rob the cop.

The plan was that his associate was to hit the cop in the head with a sap, knock him out and rob him. The cop, however, was armed with a gun and was being monitored on a radio. When he got hit, he was knocked down, but not out. He announced he was a cop, and the dope dealer said, "Oh shit, now we'll have to kill him." Fortunately, his fellow officers rescued him.

At the trial, the prosecutor wanted to make the point that the sap was truly a dangerous weapon, so he slammed it down hard on a book, resting on the counsel table. It made a good loud smack. To counter this proposition and advance his own contention that this was little more than a toy, defense counsel, during his final argument, picked it up and rapped himself rather sharply in the back of the head. The blow staggered him, buckled his knees and brought tears to his eyes. It rendered him speechless for about two and a half minutes.

Upon retiring to deliberate, gales of laughter were heard coming from the jury room. The suspect was convicted.

PENNIES FROM HEAVEN

Two Hmong ladies from the St. Paul Hmong community, about to pay a visit to the Grand Casino in Hinkley, owned by the Mille Lacs Band of Chippewa, left their gold necklaces and several hundred dollars with a fortune teller so she could bless them. This they felt would enable them to win more money.

The fortune teller blessed their money and jewelry and left town, but not necessarily in that order.

UP IN SMOKE

One night, a Mexican youth brought a friend home to stay the night and the companion went into the bedroom where the mother was sleeping and began to disrobe her. The mother woke up screaming, so the assailant jumped out a window, leaving his trousers with his billfold and ID hanging on the bedpost.

In a frantic effort to cover his foul deed, he ran home, got dressed and was walking back to the scene of the attack. The police caught him, and he explained he had been to the house in question, and had been attacked by an unknown assailant who stole his trousers and he was now heading back to warn the others in the house.

Unfortunately, for the sake of his story's credibility, he had the woman's cigarette lighter and cigarettes, which were last seen in her bedroom, in his shirt pocket. His imagination earned him a high mark, however.

~

In furtherance of this investigation, I have *copulated* a number of reports.

~

NEITHER SNOW NOR DARK OF NIGHT

Once, two guys decided to rob a Dunkin Donut shop on University Avenue during a snowstorm. They used a taxicab as their mode of transportation both to and from the scene. When they arrived, they told the driver to sit outside and wait. He did so and a few minutes later they came running out and jumped in the cab, ordering him to drive off.

The police were on their trail almost immediately. The guys put a gun to the cabbies head and told him if they were caught, they'd shoot him. Then, they ordered him to make a high speed turn on Snelling Avenue. He complied, but lost control and managed to roll the cab as he did so. The two jumped out and ran.

One was caught immediately by a police dog, but the other ran down an alley. He spotted a brick wall about four feet high and vaulted it. Imagine his surprise when he fell into a newly dug basement, in the dark, breaking both ankles. He too, was tracked down and caught.

Meanwhile, back at the scene of the rollover, more cops arrived to assist and the police dog abandoned the robber and started biting them.

*   *   *   *   *

We had another such case, where two robbers tried to make a getaway on some very slippery streets. That driver also lost control of his car as it rounded a corner and slid into a snow bank. His companion said at this point the guy pulled a gun, but as he did so, he accidentally shot himself in the leg. Thus frustrated he exclaimed, "Oh damn!" and then shot himself in the head.

Is it any wonder the crime rate here in Minnesota drops right through the floor in February?

SCUFF MARK

Eugene "Scuff Mark" M went into a very tough bar habituated by a motorcycle gang. His plan was to rob the place. He used the old "hand in the pocket pretend it's a pistol" ruse. When the bartender put the money on the bar, Scuff Mark used his *gun* hand to reach for it. He was immediately set upon by the patrons — and that's how he earned his nickname.

*   *   *   *   *

Scuff Mark was a repeater, whose specialty was robbery. One time, while he was out on parole and actually had a job, he importuned his employer to drive him to a bar where he said a guy owed him some money.

The employer, being a good natured sort, drove Scuff Mark to the bar where he waited, unknowingly, while Scuff Mark committed another robbery.

THREE TIMES BURNED

We once had a fire at a suburban nursery. A very large greenhouse and the adjoining office were destroyed by a disgruntled employee who poured gasoline all over the place and lit it up.

The next day he failed to appear for work. But a few days later, he appeared heavily bandaged, looking like a mummy and fire investigators asked him what happened. He said his sister was having a baby in a small town in Northern Wisconsin and it was thought she might die, so he had to go there just in case. He said during the night he was riding a motorcycle with his brother-in-law, which tipped over on a gravel road and he was both scraped up from the gravel and burned from coming into contact with the hot muffler.

Investigators called the Wisconsin town and learned there was no sister having a baby nor did this guy show up for any treatment at any of their local doctor's offices or the hospital.

Because the investigators were not satisfied with his story, they continued working on the case. They turned to his girlfriend, who stated he told her he was out at a bar and met a Marine home on leave who wanted to go out for a steak, so he suggested Stuart Anderson's Cattle Company. When they got to the parking lot there, they were suddenly set upon by two guys who apparently had it in for the Marine. When our hero tried to intervene, they squirted lighter fluid all over him and set him on fire. He did not report this to police in fear the two assailants might be members of the Mafia and would come after him.

The morning after the fire, he reported to a local Doctor's office, where he told the receptionist he had been burned as a result of the explosion of a charcoal grill where he lived with his girlfriend. She denied such a thing ever happened.

By this time, his girlfriend began to sense this guy was a looser, so she kicked him out. He went back to the home of his former landlady and told her he was out driving around on the evening of the fire and as he drove by his place of employment, he sensed something was wrong, so he went in to investigate. Just at that point, the building exploded in flames.

He should have been a Hollywood script writer.

WHEN YOUR TIME ISN'T UP — IT ISN'T UP

Occasionally, a guy will try to commit suicide by police. One such nut called police to complain there was a man with a gun in a particular house. Then he got in bed and covered up with a blanket. When police arrived to investigate, he pulled a gun and pointed it at them. For some reason, they didn't shoot him.

A few weeks later, while out on bail, he gave it another try. This time, he opened the gas on the stove and laid down to go to what he thought would be a permanent sleep. For some reason, he woke up and, forgetting the gas was on, decided to have a smoke. He blew the house to kingdom come, but survived once again.

* * * * *

Another suicide decided to use gasoline. He poured about a quart of gasoline into each of four plastic wastebaskets and placed on in each corner of his living room. He waited about ten minutes and then stood in the middle of the room and lit a match. The ensuing explosion blew him clear through the picture window and his efforts met with success, but not until he had been about one week in the hospital, suffering from horrible burns.

ONCE IS NEVER ENOUGH

Occassionally, one runs across a situation where a victim takes the law into his own hands and often gets away with it, probably rightfully so. I recall a case in Florida which made national news when the owner of a dry cleaning establishment had had it. He was getting burglarized over and over again, and all the customers' clothing would be stolen. It was getting to be bad for business.

The burglaries always occurred with the same MO. The burglar would cut a hole in the rooftop and come down through the ceiling. One night as he left work, our shop owner rigged a metal box spring mattress under the spot where the roof kept getting cut open and used the simple expedient of hooking the two bare ends of an electric cord to the box spring. Then he plugged the cord into the wall outlet. That night, the burglar came through the roof and electrocuted himself.

A nationally syndicated newscast interviewed their legal expert, who assured them the shop owner was guilty of some form of homicide, but a grand jury decided differently.

The reason I tell this story, is nearly every experienced prosecutor has had similar situations with similar results. One time, we had a citizen who got his car broken into several times and decided to stay awake to see if he could do something about it. sure enough, the thief showed up and the citizen shot him, wounding, but not killing him.

I presented the case to the grand jury. Grand jurors are permitted to ask questions of the witnesses, unlike a trial jury. The citizen came and testified to the numerous break-ins and thefts of valuable equipment from his car. One member of the grand jury asked him what he did after he shot the intruder. "I called the police," was the reply.

I knew the case was in trouble when the juror asked him, "Why didn't you shoot him again?"

POT LUCK

Another case which always amazed me was a robbery of a number of people gathered in a home to play poker. This was a very high stakes poker game with several prominent citizens involved. Moreover, it was a game which was held at least once a month.

One of the participants, Mike G, turned out to be a consistent loser, and there is a school of thought that he engineered a robbery to make up for his losses. During the game, two masked intruders, wearing coveralls, came in and stuck the place up. The homeowner's daughter was able to discern what was going on and called the sheriff from an upstairs telephone. As the robbers were about to leave, they saw several sheriff's cars surrounding the area. They decided to take the homeowner's wife, his two teenaged sons and the above-mentioned Mike G as hostages. They made it to Mike G's car, a '74 Pontiac Bonneville, and made a run for it.

The sheriff gave chase and radioed for help to all other nearby police departments. One cop in the small town of Hugo, a few miles north of the Twin Cities, fired a 12 gauge shotgun at the flank of the car as it flew by, inflicting a wound on the car with the neatest bulls-eye pattern you ever saw. They made it to the next suburb north, Forest Lake, and the deputy chasing the car burned out the motor of his AMC Ambassador.

While in Forest Lake, they limped the wounded car into the yard of a house occupied by a Federal Alcohol, Tobacco and Firearms agent. They wound up shooting, but not killing him, and stealing his new Ford. They started south on Interstate 35, where the Minnesota Highway Patrol got on their tail. While going at speeds of 95 and 100 miles-per-hour, the highway patrolman in the passenger side of the car started blazing away with a 12-gauge, loaded with 00 buckshot — firing at the getaway car filled with two robbers, three hostages and Mike G. All told, I counted 19 holes in the car. Finally, they shot out the tires and the car ground to a halt. What's so unfathomable about this case is that nobody was hurt, even though all the widows were blown out of the car.

A few weeks later, Mike G was severely beaten and badly wounded. He claimed he didn't know who did it, but a few weeks after that, the home where the game was held burned down. That case was never solved either.

~

The victim spoke no English. We were told by a neighbor he had recently *defecated* from Russia.

~

THE ADVENTURES OF MIKE AND ROLLIE

One of the legendary figures of the Ramsey County Attorney's Office was Mike Kinkead, County Attorney during the 1930's. He was an icon at the time, an Irishman who could not be defeated in what was a predominantly Irish town. He was later appointed to a judgeship and spent the rest of his career in that capacity.

The most famous of his exploits concerned his trip to Ireland. One day in the late 1930's, he received word that some criminal wanted in St. Paul had been captured somewhere in Ireland. Even though it was not a particularly serious crime, Mike decided he and his first assistant, Rollie (also an Irishman), probably better go to Ireland (at county expense) to attend to the extradition.

At least two stories about the trip, perhaps apocryphal, circulate to this day. One has it that, just as Mike and his companion were about to board the ship, a telegram bellhop came through the crowd loudly yelling, "Mike Kinkead, Mike Kinkead, telegram for Mike Kinkead."

"I'll be taking that, me boy," said Mike.

He unfolded it and read to the effect the prisoner had escaped and he needn't come over as he had planned. Mike is said to have calmly folded the telegram back up, handed it back to the messenger and said, "You've got the wrong Mike Kinkead, me lad."

They proceeded to Ireland and, sure enough, the prisoner had escaped. This necessitated a thorough search of nearly every pub in Ireland to see if they could find him, all to no avail.

Downhearted (I'm sure) they returned home. Upon landing in New York, they chanced upon a man from St. Paul who knew them, at least by reputation (who didn't?).

Their newfound companion suggested a night on the town; he'd show them around. Unwilling to offend a prospective voter, or any of his family members, Mike and Rollie graciously accepted. For whatever reason, their guide put them on to apricot brandy alexanders, which went down very smoothly.

Rollie awoke first the next morning and felt the need of a little bit more of what they had the night before. He called room service and said, "Send up six apricot brandy alexanders."

Mike was awake by now, grabbed the phone and announced, "The selfish son-of-a-bitch thinks only of himself. Send up twelve."

NOTORIOUS CASES OF RAMSEY COUNTY

At this point I'm going to turn away from the stupid, amusing and bizarre to discuss in, detail, some of the cases of interest our office has tried. Though they are a bit more hard-edged than the previous section of this book, I include them because they are the most frequently asked about cases occurring during my tenure in office. To recount them verbatim from case records would be an exercise in tedium for myself and the reader. Therefore, these are condensed but accurate accounts.

* * * * *

The T Eugene Thompson murder case was probably the biggest case our office handled during my tenure. It was prosecuted by William B Randall, the Ramsey County Attorney. Assisting him was Steven J Maxwell. Maxwell, in turn, tried the companion case of one of the accomplices. I use the names here because these cases were both reported in the opinions of the Minnesota Supreme Court.

The T Eugene Thompson case probably starts with the disappearance of a local restaurateur in the fall of 1961. He had just come back from federal prison and his wife feared him. She had also found a new boyfriend. The restaurateur's body was not found for several months and, when it finally was found, it was because the wife of the man who was to become T Eugene's accomplice told St. Paul police that the restaurateur had been killed by her husband at their suburban Anoka County home, at the insistence of the man's wife. The informant further stated that her husband and the widow's new boyfriend had done the job. The informant had grown disenchanted with her husband, needless to say.

They took the body and deposited it in the woods, hoping it would be found by some hunters so the insurance proceeds could be collected, but that hadn't worked out. Therefore, on the next night after the informant gave this information, the informant's husband and the widow's new boyfriend were going to drive by the site and reconnoiter it. If the coast seemed to be clear the following night, they were going to pick the body up, put it in the trunk of a car and reposition it so it could be found and the insurance collected.

St. Paul officers found the body and stationed themselves in the woods to see what would happen. Sure enough, that night the car pulled up and reconnoitered the situation and drove away. The plan was to wait until the following night and catch the two red-handed as they carried the corpse to the car.

At this point, the St. Paul Police notified the Anoka County authorities who thought it would be a desecration to allow it to lie in the field one more night. They recovered it and announced to the press the fact that the missing restaurateur's body had been recovered. As Captain Barkely of the St. Paul Police Department put it, "We just solved a missing person case and Anoka County has an unsolved homicide."

The Anoka County sheriff arrested the informant's husband and his companion and held them for three days, trying to sweat a confession out of them, but with no success. They finally had to release the two.

T Eugene Thompson was a lawyer in St. Paul, about 33 years old with a reasonably successful practice. Among other things, he was the prosecuting attorney for the City of North St. Paul, a suburb. He was married to a local girl, the daughter of a successful plumbing contractor, had three children and a very nice home in the toney Highland Park area of St. Paul. He also had a girlfriend who was anxious for him to divorce so she could marry him.

The man arrested in the death of the restaurateur came to him with the idea they should sue Anoka County for false arrest and Thompson agreed. To sustain such a suit, the plaintiff must show the authorities did not have sufficient "probable cause" to make the arrest. In Minnesota, in order to start a lawsuit against the county at that time, the plaintiff had to give notice of his intent to do so. As Thompson served the notice, he was told by the Anoka County authorities they had sufficient probable cause to make the arrest and showed him the statement given by the wife. Under the law, even though her testimony could not be used against him in court, it was sufficient to constitute probable cause to arrest.

By revealing this information, the wife was placed at some risk and had to be given immediate refuge elsewhere. After Thompson learned that, it is believed he turned to his client and explained the lawsuit idea had some flaws. It is also believed that at this time, he hatched an alternate plan for his client to make some money, for it was then he immediately started taking out huge sums of life insurance on his wife. He also told his girlfriend to give him one year and, within that time, he would divorce his wife and have enough money to live on for the rest of his life.

Thompson bought what is known as *term* insurance to cover his wife. This is relatively inexpensive, especially for young people, because it only covers a person for one year. Also, much of it was *double indemnity,* providing additional coverage if the death was accidental. A few hundred-thousand dollars worth were purchased this way. Then he got even greedier and bought several hundred-thousand dollars worth of *accidental death* insurance. This covers one only for accidental deaths and is comparable in cost to the sort of policy one buys at the airport in case of a plane crash resulting in death. It has the least expensive premium for the most amount of coverage. In all, Thompson accumulated $1,000,000 worth of term and accidental death coverage for his wife over the next twelve months.

Meanwhile, some preparations had to be made back at the homestead. A barking dog had to be gotten rid of and a *princess* style telephone set had to be removed from the bedroom.

Thompson was apparently unaware his client had decided to subcontract the job, and was casting about for a hit man. He discussed the plan with a trio of burglars, none of whom really wanted to do it. They did, however, put him in touch with one Dick A.

Mrs. Thompson was killed by an intruder about 7:00 AM one morning in March of 1963. She did not die immediately, but made her way, nude, to a neighbor's house, where her only words were, "A man, a man." She was taken to the hospital but died within a matter of hours. She had numerous stab wounds all over her upper torso, and some small, but deep, scuff marks on the back of her skull. The blade of a paring knife was broken off in her neck.

Upon examination of the home, police noted some unusual features. Most prominent was a tub full of clean water. There was, of course, extensive blood splattering, especially in the stairway leading to the second floor bedroom area, and there was also a piece of rubber hose wrapped around a steel cable which was folded and tied at the bottom so it resembled the outline of a paddle-ball racquet. Also, there was a peculiar piece of plastic about two inches long, which had an unusual design.

The plastic was examined by criminalist, Ted Elzerman, of the St. Paul Police Crime Lab, and after a little study, he concluded it had broken off a custom made handle of a World War II German Luger. Armed with this information, the police produced a picture of what such a weapon would have looked like and distributed it to all local papers, inquiring if anybody knew about it. Shortly after, a local man told police such a gun had been stolen from him in a house burglary.

On the day Mrs. Thompson was killed, Captain Barkley, of the St. Paul Homicide Division, spoke to Thompson at the hospital, where he had been summoned. Thompson carried a briefcase and, for whatever peculiar reason, Barkley inquired if he could look in it and Thompson gave permission. The only things of note were an envelope with "enough stamps on it to go around the world three times," as Barkely put it, and $5,000 in cash. In those days, that was a very large sum to carry around (it would be the equivalent of $30,000 to $40,000 today). Barkely asked about it and Thompson told him he always carried that much cash. When asked why a clean tub of water would be in the home, Thompson answered that he was going to take a bath that morning, but decided against it and forgot to drain the tub.

A few weeks after Mrs. Thompson was killed, and shortly after the gun display had been placed in the paper, two of the three criminals by Thompson's client, tried their hand at an armed robbery which was not hugely successful. By a quirky stroke of fate, one made his first appearance in court one day, and the second one appeared the next day. The first one drew a lenient judge and prosecutor and a fairly low bail was set. The second one appeared before a much harsher judge. I happened to be the prosecutor and, feeling spunky, I asked for a very high bail, together with a speech about what a danger this man was to the community. The judge gave him an exceptionally high bail.

This spooked the second robber, who, knowing he and his partner were the ones who had stolen the gun, put two and two together and got five. He thought his partner had probably turned him in on the gun burglary job thereby getting his bail lowered, and that

I was aware of this and had demanded the high bail for him. He requested to see the County Attorney.

That morning he told the tale of how Thompson's client (the husband of the informant on the restaurateur's case) and a companion had approached him and his associate shortly before Mrs. Thompson was killed, wanting to know if they would undertake such a job. He explained the client and his companion wanted to know if they knew how to wire a car with dynamite, so it would blow up when the starter was turned. It was explained that it was necessary to make this look like an accidental death "for insurance purposes." The client and his companion even wanted the car to blow up at a time when Mrs. Thompson would be driving some other ladies to a bridge game, so no one would know which of them had been the exact target of the attack. They declined, but agreed to try to find some other candidate.

They eventually came up with a third man, who, while he wouldn't do the job, could find someone that would. A few days later, after some meetings in a bar, the plan finally came together. Present at that meeting were one or more of our burglar friends, Thompson's client and Dick A. The burglar had given the gun to Dick A, but told him to use it in an emergency only. They drove by the Thompson home to show him where she lived and acquaint him with the area.

The plan was explained this way. The death had to look like an accident for insurance purposes. Dick A was told the back door would be left unlocked on the day this was to happen. He was to take the rubber hose *whopper* and go in the kitchen and open the door to the basement and wait on the top step. At 7:00 AM. the phone would ring and the only phone in the house would be situated in the kitchen. Mrs. Thompson would answer it with her back to the basement door. Dick A was then to come through the door and hit her, hard, in the back of the head with the whopper. He was then to take her to the upstairs bathroom where there would be a tub full of water. He was to disrobe her and place her in the tub and hold her under the water until she drowned. Then he was to leave her to be found when her husband or children came home later that day.

Police quickly rounded up Thompson's accomplice. The burglar quickly confirmed the story told by the first burglar.

About this time, the story of the $1,000,000 worth of life insurance came to light. A visit was paid to T Eugene Thompson's summer home on the St. Croix River, where a piece of garden hose was noted to have a hunk cut off the end. It was examined by criminalist Elzerman, and found to be cut in such a way as to exactly match the cut in the hose left at the scene — the whopper, as it came to be known.

Further evidence surfaced about that time. Thompson's secretary was interviewed and told police on the day of the death, Thompson, for the first and only time she ever recalled, came in at about five minutes before seven that morning, even calling her attention to the exact time. Then, after removing his overcoat and hat, he directed her to dial his home, get Mrs. Thompson on the line and notify him immediately when she answered so he could talk to her. The secretary did so and stated this was the only time she had ever been given such instructions.

Armed with this information, our office quickly got an indictment against Thompson's client and Dick A. We felt we needed more on Thompson and waited to see what could be developed. The girlfriend surfaced and told of the conversation where Thompson said he would marry her in one year and they would have plenty of money.

Dick A decided at this point, confession would be good for his soul. His attorney informed Bill Randall and a conversation was arranged. Dick A reiterated the story, and told that as he was trying to get Mrs. Thompson undressed to place her in the waiting tub of water, she came to and fought like a tiger. He hit her in the back of the head several times with the Luger, with the result that part of the handle broke off. She made it to the kitchen, where the fight continued. In desperation, Dick A picked up a paring knife and started stabbing her with it. The handle broke off when he stabbed her in the neck, and he ran from the scene.

Shortly after Mrs. Thompson's death, the trunk of Thompson's car was searched and a princess telephone was found. It had previously been in the upstairs bedroom of the house. Thompson explained it wasn't working and he was going to take it in for repair. The phone company checked it out and it worked perfectly.

Friends and neighbors of the Thompsons also told police the family dog had been gotten rid of shortly before the murder. Thompson said it made a mess on the carpeting. Thompson gave testimony at the first grand jury hearing at which the client and Anderson were indicted and explained he had taken out the $1,000,000 worth of life insurance because he had a *premonition* his wife was going to die accidentally.

Two well known movies had shown in St. Paul shortly before the time Mrs. Thompson was killed. One was *Diabolique* and the other was *Dial M For Murder*. *In Diabolique*, two women conspire to place their unconscious husband-lover in a bathtub full of water, weigh him down and drown him. In *Dial M For Murder*, a man hires another to kill his wife as she answers the phone. If we combine these two plots, we have the plan to kill Mrs. Thompson. It is not known whether Thompson saw these two movies.

Thompson and his client were both convicted of Murder in the First Degree and sentenced to life. Each served about 18 to 19 years. Dick A pled guilty and served the same amount of time. After his plea and sentence, however, the Minnesota prison authorities placed him in the same prison as Thompson and his client. Within a month or two, he recanted his testimony against them. At a motion for a new trial, however, he returned to his original testimony and explained his life had been threatened in prison unless he changed his story. After that, he was placed in an out-of-state prison.

*   *   *   *   *

One of my biggest murder trials involved one Robert P. The victim was a 13-year-old girl, Susan M, who, on the night she was killed, was baby-sitting for a woman who happened to be a sometimes girlfriend of Robert P.

The mostly nude, mutilated body of Susan M was found on the ice rink of a neighborhood playground on the East Side of St. Paul, by two women who were looking for the St. Paul Winter Carnival Medallion, which is worth some money if found. What was left of her clothing was in considerable disarray. Her face had been terribly torn by what appeared to be a studded snow tire being driven over it. There were also tracks from a studded snow tire on the ice of the rink, leading away from the point where her body was found.

The coroner's autopsy revealed she had been raped — sperm was found inside her vagina. Additionally, an instrument (the Doctor theorized something similar to a tire iron) had been inserted in her vagina and pushed in so far it penetrated her liver. Her skull was fractured on the top and back by a similar instrument. Finally, it was noted that her body had probably been run over by a car, because, among the other injuries, there was a large smear of grease on her thigh.

Two young boys, about 12-years-old, had run away from home on the night in question and were staying at the home where Susan M was baby-sitting. They said a knock came to the door and, fearing it was the authorities looking for them, they hid in the bedroom. They heard a man speaking to Susan, saying that the woman for whom she baby-sat was drunk and out in the car and he needed her help getting the householder inside. Susan left the house and that was the last anyone saw of her until she was found on the ice rink.

When police interviewed the woman for whom Susan baby-sat, they learned she had been at an East Side bar known as the Payne Avenue Rec. There she encountered the suspect, Robert P, together with some companions. Police recalled that suspicion had fallen on P for a similar baby-sitter attack within the past year. In that case, he also met a woman whom he had dated at a bar, knew she had a baby-sitter at her house, went to the house and enticed the baby-sitter outside on the pretext he needed help with his car. He raped the girl after hitting her in the back of the head, knocking her out. In that case, however, he let her go without killing her. Unfortunately, her identification was not as positive as we would have liked for the purpose of trying him.

The previous episode, however, led police to believe Robert P was responsible for this event, especially as one of his companions that night explained that Robert P disappeared shortly after he saw a former girlfriend at the bar. At that point I was called upon to prepare a search warrant. In the search warrant we sought Robert P's car, to search for any trace of Susan M's presence, a jacket he was said to be wearing that night — for the same reason and some white adhesive tape of a type used to bind Susan M's wrists.

Not too long before this case, the Supreme Court of the United States decided *Miranda v. Arizona,* which required police to warn suspects of their right to remain silent, to have an attorney, including a free one if he was indigent, and the fact that whatever he said could be used against him in court. This warning was only required, however, *if the suspect was in custody.* For that reason, and because I felt it was necessary to get Robert P connected firmly to the car and the coat he was wearing that evening, I gave very explicit directions to the detectives — execute the search warrant to interview Robert P in the setting of his own home, even with his parents present, and inquire if anyone else used his car that night and if he was wearing his jacket that night. I also instructed them not to take him into custody in any circumstance. This worked well, for Robert P acknowledged that he and only he drove his car that night, and that he and only he wore that jacket that night.

Police also found some white adhesive tape in the bathroom, which they took. They noted some scratches on the back of his hands. He explained they were the result of his dog nipping him for playing too rough. They also found, quite unexpectedly and by accident, an approximately one-inch stack of handwritten material in Robert P's bedroom, which detailed plans for kidnapping, raping, torturing and murdering women. They took this too.

The car was examined the very night it was seized by police criminalist Mike Alfultis. On the underside of the car he observed, photographed and gathered several strands of hair for further analysis. He also took some sample of grease from the underside of the car. On the interior of the car, he also noted some strands of hair and gathered some fibers from the floor mat. He also noted there was no tire iron in the car.

Alfultis examined the jacket recovered from the house and said to be worn by Robert P on the evening in question. He found, particularly in the pockets, very small fibers, similar to those contained in the dress Susan M had worn on that evening. The tape from the home had the same number of fibers per inch as the used to bind Susan M's wrists and it was the same width as that used.

Alfultis noted, also, some dog hairs on the dress of Susan M and the jacket of the defendant. He inquired of the detectives who had been at the home, whether they had seen a dog and was told yes — and that Robert P had even complained the dog had nipped him. Robert P's parents were asked to give permission to police to recover a sample of the dog's hair for comparison purposes and they readily consented.

These were the results of the Alfultis examinations:

The dog hair of the Robert P household dog matched hairs found on Susan M's dress and Robert P's jacket.

Grease from the underside of Robert P's car and from Susan M's body was compared spectroscopically and found to be identical. Such grease will pick up elements from road spray and other environmental sources and these can be detected with a mass spectrometer, which the St. Paul Police Crime Lab had just acquired.

Hair from the underside and interior of the car matched Susan M's. While the hair did not lend itself to a positive analysis, many points of comparison were noted; the shaft diameter, the scale structure and the color. In her case, the color was convincing because she bleached her hair and the roots were growing out darker. The extent of un-bleached growth on the hairs from the car and those from her head were identical.

Fibers on Susan M's dress matched the carpeting of the car.

The dress Susan M wore that night had a fabric which consisted of a thread with three stands — one brown, one black and one white. Each of these, in turn, had three threads — one cotton and two rayon. The small strands in Robert P's jacket pocket were examined microscopically and photographed. The color photograph was then blown up and the strands looked about as big around as a clothesline rope.

Another similar photograph was made of the strands from her dress and the results were unmistakable even to the untrained eye — a brown strand, a black strand and a white strand, each containing one thread of cotton and two of rayon.

Robert P's car was found to contain studded tires of an unusual pattern. A rubber cast was made of their pattern and compared with the pattern left on the ice rink where Susan M had been found. In fact, the car had sat on that ice for a period of time and had left an impression of the entire width of its tread, which had some slight defects also found on the tires of Robert P's car.

Before we could begin the trial, we had to have a hearing before the judge to rule on the admissibility of our evidence. We were stunned when he ruled that, although there was sufficient probable cause in the search warrant to justify seizure of Robert P's jacket, there was not sufficient probable cause to justify the seizure of his car. Further, he ruled out the use of the adhesive tape found in P's home because, he said, it should have been characterized as "surgical tape." He also ruled the writings found in Robert P's bedroom could not be used because they had not been mentioned in the warrant. How could we mention them when we had no idea they existed at that time? Since then we have usually included a phrase in our warrants allowing us to search for writings which might be of evidentiary value to the case.

Very fortunately, our office had successfully lobbied the State Legislature to allow us to appeal such rulings made before trial and we did so immediately. Although it took almost a year to complete, the Minnesota Supreme Court reversed the trial judge on nearly all his rulings and allowed our evidence in. They only thing they excluded were the writings.

During this year, however, some interesting things occurred. In the spring, when the snow was thawing, a hardware store owner, whose business was located near the scene of the crime, noted a leak in his roof. He went to the top to examine and found an army blanket with Robert P's name embroidered on it. Wrapped in the blanket was a tire iron of the same type normally found in Robert P's car.

Also, the sheriff noted that Robert P had used an unusually large amount of paper while in the county jail, and upon searching his cell found voluminous writings of the same character as previously noted, describing kidnapping, raping, torturing and killing women.

Once again, we began trial, unfortunately with the same judge. This time he ruled the writings seized from the jail cell were not the product of an illegal search and seizure. The trial went smoothly, with all the evidence coming in, except that the judge ruled during the trial that we could not use the writings seized in the jail cell as they were not relevant. Because this ruling came during the middle of the trial, no appeal was available.

At the trial, Robert P testified he thought someone stole his car on the evening of the crime because it was not in the same place where he parked it before going into the bar. He had to admit, however, he never noted this when talking to police, nor did he note any damage to indicate the car was hot-wired in any way. He also acknowledged he had the only keys to the car that entire night and he admitted the jacket we recovered was the one he wore that night. The value of our non-custodial, unwarned interview had paid off. After one day of deliberation, he was convicted of First Degree Murder.

After the conviction, our office initiated a *Psychopathic Personality* hearing in Probate Court. There, all his fantasy writings were admitted and he was adjudged to be a psychopathic personality and ordered confined to the Minnesota State Security Hospital at St. Peter. There he continued to write his fantasies out, and at one point commented to the effect, "These fools have lowered my security status and it will only be a matter of time before I can escape." He was even allowed to marry and spend a night outside the grounds on his honeymoon.

The marriage did not last long. The woman was a self appointed social worker at the security hospital and became infatuated with him. She divorced him after a short time and he wrote, threatening her. He then *did* escape. The then Chief of St. Paul Police, Dick Rowan, ordered a squad to her home, which was in the suburb of Forest Lake. Sure enough, they found him hiding there in a closet with a knife, waiting for his wife to return home.

* * * * *

A most unusual homicide confronted the Ramsey County Sheriff's Office one morning in early June of 1981. A 28-year-old male student at the University of Minnesota was found dead in his bed with head wounds so severe it almost looked as if he had been shot at close range with a 12-gauge shotgun. Later, the medical examiner determined that he had been beaten many times, on the head, with a steel pipe or rod.

The student lived at home with his somewhat invalid mother and a sister in a very out of the way, quiet neighborhood in a second tier suburb of St. Paul. He had a girlfriend, Urmi D, who was a graduate student in Physics at the University. When she first came to the United States, a fellow graduate student in Physics, William C, tried to engage her romantically. Because he had so few social skills, he was unable to interest her. The closest he came was to invite her to his home for Thanksgiving, and because she was interested in learning something of American customs, she accepted. Other than that, she had as little to do with him as possible, which was also the case with other women he encountered.

He was of very slight build, a mousy sort of person whose only accomplishment to date had been to graduate number two in his university class, as a Physics major. He was not doing particularly well, however, in his graduate studies at the University and it developed he had been a very definite overachiever.

Urmi D, after the death of her boyfriend, took up with another university student. Pretty soon the place he lived in started catching fire (five times — all minor fires started under the porch). Then his parents' home in Fairbault, about 50 miles away, caught fire, as did his grandparents' home in the same town.

Because the new boyfriend had a dispute with his landlord, he speculated that the landlord was trying to burn him out, so he moved to a different place. Imagine his surprise when it, too, caught fire.

A friend of Urmi's, a fellow graduate student from India, put two and two together and told her the same guy who killed her boyfriend was doubtless one and the same who was setting fires to her new boyfriend's place. He opined it was the same guy who had tried unsuccessfully to date her. She dismissed this because the guy was such a mouse in her opinion.

Her new boyfriend, however, rigged a rather sophisticated electronic alarm system and sure enough, the next night it went off. Urmi happened to be visiting at the time and they both went outside. There was her would-be-boyfriend coming out from under the porch where he had materials for another fire.

Upon their arrival, the first officer asked him his name and he responded he wanted to see a lawyer. Later that day, he gave a complete confession to an investigator, admitting to both setting the fires and killing the first boyfriend. His first comment, however, created very serious legal problems, because the Supreme Court of the United States had just decided *Edwards v. Arizona* in which they held, "once a defendant asks for an attorney, police may not thereafter question him unless he initiates the conversation," which in this case he didn't.

It is of such problems that plea bargains are made. Without his confession, which stood an excellent chance of being suppressed, we had only his attraction for Urmi and the fact that one of her boyfriends was killed and the other one kept catching fire. Also a three-foot long piece of iron was found in the trunk of his car, which, although cleaned off, could have been the murder weapon.

Through his attorney, he offered to plead guilty to a lesser charge if he could be guaranteed a maximum sentence of 15 years. This was accepted.

*   *   *   *   *

Burke L and his wife Rose lived together off and on in California, Massachusetts and finally Minnesota, in the small suburb of North St. Paul, where she was from originally. There was a considerable history of wife beating and she had been to the hospital at least twice as a result such beatings, one time each in California and Massachusetts.

In St. Paul, they had gone to marriage counseling and things still didn't seem to work out. Each had been married once before and Rose had a son by her first husband. The son also suffered physical abuse, but to a lesser degree than his mother. On the first day of school in 1983, he left his mother and stepfather at about 7:45 AM to go to school. She was perfectly fine at the time.

Burke had just returned to the household from New Jersey, where he had lived during a trial separation for about six or eight months. Rose would not permit him to stay in the house for fear of more beatings, although he did stay for two nights while he located another place. He located an apartment about two blocks away and, on the morning Rose was found dead, Burke arrived to inspect it at 8:25. The caretaker took note of the precise time on his nearly new quartz watch, which he said was highly accurate. The reason he noted the time was, he hadn't quite finished cleaning the place up and he did not expect Burke until 9:00 AM. He even commented on the fact that Burke had arrived 25 minutes early.

Burke inspected the place for two or three minutes and walked home, which took another two minutes as later verified by a detective who walked it at a normal pace. Burke claimed when he got home, he climbed a tree as he had seen Rose's son do, to get to the top of a motor home they owned. He claimed Rose had mentioned the roof had a leak in it and he wished to inspect it. Then, he claimed, he went back down the tree and went in the house. He said he couldn't find Rose right away, so he called out and looked for her. He said he found her in the bathtub full of water, face down. He pulled her out, he said, and ran next door for help.

The neighbor lady called the police at 9:33 AM according to the timed tape recording. All of what I described happened in eight minutes; at least we can fix a starting time at 8:25 AM when Burke arrived to inspect the apartment and the ending time at 8:33 AM-when police were called.

When police arrived, they found Burke on the floor giving mouth-to-mouth to Rose. She was immediately taken to St. Paul Ramsey Hospital and placed on artificial respiration. She never regained consciousness and died.

The first officer noted no bruises on Rose's body, even though she was nude. A detective was called and found a very curious scene in the bathroom. The tub was full of muddy water, which could have come from Burke's shoes if he got in the tub to pull her out, as he claimed. He had to walk a rather muddy path to the apartment and back. However, when he drained the water, he found submerged, a ladies' electrical hair curler — the kind that has heated spindles upon which curlers are placed. It also had a light for the mirror contained inside the top cover. He also noted the electrical cord for it extending from the wall outlet across the small bathroom in a general direction toward the tub giving the appearance of having been plugged into the appliance. Burke was later heard to tell the neighbor lady that it looked like Rose had some kind of an accident as a hair curler had been found in the tub under where he had found her.

We came next to the pathologist with the critical question, "How did she die? Was she drowned or electrocuted?" The pathologist and two others who were also consulted said there is no medical way to tell the difference. Most people believe when one drowns, the lungs fill up with water. Most people are wrong on this point. As one pathologist explained to me, "God never intended mankind to breathe water, because we don't have gills. What happens is, an apparatus in your throat, the glottis, closes down like a damper so you can't breath water into your lungs. This reflex simply shuts down the airway and you die because you suffocate, just as you would if someone held their hand over your mouth and nose."

"Surely," I asked "You can tell whether or not she was electrocuted?" The answer came back an unequivocal, "Maybe."

"The most common symptom of household voltage electrocution is what is called an entry burn wound. At the point of entry of the electricity we usually, but not always, find a reddening of the flesh in a star shaped pattern due to the heating caused by the incoming current. However, if the electrocuted person were under water, this phenomenon might not occur for two reasons — first, there would not be a definite point of entry because the current would presumably diffuse through the entire volume of water and, second, even if there was a defined point of entry, the surrounding water would cool it so as not to leave an entry burn wound. Again, the mechanism of death would be the cessation of the heartbeat and anatomically there is no way under the circumstances to differentiate between this and drowning."

Compounding the problem was the fact that this particular house, which was rather old, had some months previous to the event, a defect in that if you touched it anywhere on the outside (aluminum siding) or touched any of the water faucets, you received a terrific electrical shock. This had been fixed by a competent electrician, however.

The fact the first officer on the scene noted no bruises on the body was also puzzling, because the pathologist who performed the autopsy noted twelve distinct, deep bruises distributed all over her body. Her son, who left her at 7:45 AM, said she had no noticeable bruising at that time.

I asked the pathologist how we could account for these bruises. His answer was they were so widely dispersed and deep, they could only be accounted for by the fact that she had been beaten at or just before the time of her death. I asked if he could rule out accidental death and he replied for sure, as accidents didn't leave bruises in the somewhat sheltered positions hers were located; such as the interior aspects of the arms and legs and the palm of the hand.

Then I asked why the first officer on the scene failed to notice these, and the pathologist had no answer. An idea hit me a little later and I asked the doctor to tell me how one becomes bruised. He explained that an impact causes small capillary blood vessels to break and these leak blood into the surrounding tissue, which shows up as a bruise.

"What would happen if the person were killed very shortly after suffering this impact?" I asked. I was told there probably wouldn't be a visible bruise, because after the heart stops beating, no more blood is being pumped to leak out to the surrounding tissue. Then I asked what would happen if the person were dead, but placed on a respirator which artificially pumped the blood throughout the body, as Rose was. That, I was told, would account for bruising which showed up later, as the artificially induced pressure would cause the bruise to manifest itself.

At the hospital, during efforts to resuscitate Rose, there were noted on Burke's neck, three long scratch marks. The detective asked how those occurred and was told it happened when Burke climbed the tree to inspect the top of the motor home, as mentioned. Later the detective met Burke at the house and tried, himself, to climb the tree. He could do so only with great difficulty. Further, he noted there was a ladder about 25 feet away, plainly visible through a garage door.

In the meantime, Rose's father noted there was a tread pattern, of the same type tennis shoes Burke was wearing on the fateful morning, on the bumper of the motor home and also on the ledge at the bottom of its windshield. Unfortunately, it was not photographed at that time.

On the day of Rose's death, the next door lady came forward. She gave the detective an unopened letter and said, "Rose gave me this ten months ago. She said if anything ever happened to her, no matter if it looked like an accident, don't believe it, that Burke did it and I should give you this letter."

The outside of the envelope read *Last Will and Testament of Rose L.* Upon opening it, there was found a home grown will. It didn't exactly qualify as a will because it was not properly witnessed and simply did not meet the technical requirements for a will in Minnesota, or probably any other state. The will said something like this: In case of my death, I wish all of my property to go to my son, C. This is to make it known my husband Burke L, Social Security Number _____, has made threats against my life. In the event of my death, I authorize full opening of all my hospital records for any purpose by the authorities.

Signed this _____ day of _____, 1982

Rose L

While this could be a very damaging piece of evidence, the main problem with it was, it would not ordinarily be admissible before a jury because it was hearsay. To put this is proper perspective, hearsay is an out-of-court, unsworn statement which is being offered for the truth of what it says. The reason it is not admitted in evidence at a trial is twofold — first, it is an accusation which is not under oath and, second, there is no way a defendant can cross-examine the statement to test its truthfulness. Both these features were true of this statement.

However, the Minnesota Rules of Evidence had just been recently amended to relax some of the rigors of the hearsay rule. In addition to the standard exceptions to the rule, almost too numerous to mention, the new rules created a "catch-all" exception. To meet the requirements of this exception one had to show — 1) that it was more likely than not that the statement was true, 2) that a manifest injustice might occur if it was excluded, 3) that the statement must have been made under circumstances in which it was important to the person that he or she tell the truth and 4) that a notice must be given to the adverse party of the intention to use the statement.

The first thing I did was give the notice. At trial, the judge permitted the introduction of this evidence.

The next thing was to try to devise a way to prove exactly how Rose died. I happened to know the electrician who fixed the wiring in the house a few months before. He had been a neighbor of mine. Although he was a licensed electrician, he actually had an Electical Engineering degree and had worked for Honeywell for a number of years. In questioning him, I learned the problem with the house had been a bare electrical wire in contact with a cold water pipe. This allowed current to make the entire water system *hot* and because an outdoor water outlet came in contact with the aluminum siding, all of the siding was also *hot*. He assured me he simply replaced the problem wire and this completely solved the electrical shock problem. This had been done about one month before Rose's death. Rose also had a boyfriend during the interim who confirmed the electrical problem had been fixed.

The larger question I had for the electrician was, what if you happened to be in a tub full of water with an electrical hair curling appliance? His answer was, "Hard to say. There's not been a lot of empirical data collected in this field, as you might imagine."

At this point it crossed my mind to take all the prisoners from the Ramsey County Detention Center to Rose's to gather empirical data with her bathtub full of water and the plugged in curling device. I stifled my baser instincts and cast about for other means.

I asked my neighbor, who was going to have to be a witness anyway, if he might assist me in determining what we could figure out. We went to the house with the hair curling apparatus in hand and filled the tub with water. We placed the curler in the water and plugged it in the nearest wall socket, the one the detective saw the cord plugged in. Our expectation was we might blow a fuse, thus proving electrocution unlikely. Not only did our experiment fail to blow any fuses, the small lights on either side of the unit, which illuminated a mirror inside the cover, lit up. Further than this, the electrician did not care to venture. We did note, however, the cord was not long enough to allow the curler to rest on the bottom of the tub, where it had been found. It could only lean against the inside of the tub, dangling from its cord.

About this time, I was in the middle of a long, difficult trial in which St. Paul Police had tape recorded a conversation with a criminal. His defense attorney hired a forensic expert to examine the tape and I was given the opportunity to examine this expert. I was impressed with his credentials as an expert and with the honesty of his findings. I explained my problem to him in this case and asked if he would be willing to tackle it. He agreed.

He examined the hair curler first and gave me some unfortunate news. It was too bad that in the prior experiment we had plugged the thing in while partly submerged, because that had caused a chemical reaction to form a slight coating on the electrodes. Had we not done this, he could have examined the wire electrodes first, noted there was no coating and then submerged it while plugged in and determined that it had not been plugged in while in the tub, for this would have left a coating. This possibility was now lost.

However, we persisted and went to the house, filled the tub again and re-submerged the device, leaning as it did up against the side of the tub. Then my witness first took a yardstick and pushed against this devise to determine where the cord unplugged first — from the wall outlet or from the hair curler. As he did so on several occasions, it was noted it always unplugged from the wall outlet first, not from the unit itself. Remember, the detective found the cord plugged into the wall but unplugged from the hair curler, just the opposite of what our experiment would seem to show.

This was not sufficiently conclusive for either my expert or myself, so he took a number of readings with testing equipment while the plugged-in curler was in the tub full of water. He finally announced, "You know, I just don't think anything would happen if I just reached in the water and picked it up." Then to my amazement he did just that and said, "I don't feel a thing."

This was too good to believe, so I said, "Let me try." I did so, an I felt absolutely nothing. We then repeated this experiment and videotaped it for a jury to see at a later time. The videotape was fairly dramatic, because when the device went in the water, its lights lit up, proving there was current going through it, even though the separate light switch was not turned on. As we drew it out, the water drained from it and the lights went out. We reversed the polarity of the plug and repeated it with the same result. Finally, he touched the metal handled faucet and put his other hand in the water and this time he got a shock, but upon measuring the amount of current, he said it would be borderline as to whether or not it could kill someone. In any case, the location of the handle and the device were so far apart, it would be difficult for a woman of Rose's short stature to reach both.

Additionally, the probability of her having that device resting on the edge of a full tub of water was highly unlikely, for it was an old fashioned tub with rounded edges on the top and it would have been a very neat trick to balance it on there in the first place.

I asked my expert to explain how it was that one did not feel anything when this devise was plugged-in and in the water? His explanation was, electricity seeks its least resistant path and in this case, the path was from the switch through the short span of water to the electrodes. It would have to take a much longer and more resistant path to go from the switch, through a person's body, and then to the electrodes. Armed with this information I felt we could now demonstrate to a jury that Rose was drowned, not electrocuted. What, then, was the curler doing in the tub? I argued that it was placed there after the fact to make it look like an accident and to cover up a murder.

While we were at Rose's house, we did one more thing. Even though this was several months after the death, the footprints on the front bumper and the ledge under the windshield were still visible and appeared to match shoe treads such as those on Burke's shoes. These were now photographed. As mentioned, Burke offered the excuse he climbed on the camper to inspect for a leak Rose had complained about. Rose's son, however, testified he knew nothing of any leak, nor had he ever heard his mother mention it.

Upon examining the top, I found a leak all right. A piece of plastic in the overhead vent was broken out. It had fallen inside the vent onto a screen a couple of inches below it. The broken-out piece fit the hole in the part that remained. Better, still, the same tread mark of the same tennis shoe noted on the bumper and window ledge, was imprinted on the broken-out piece. It had a leak to be sure, but he made the leak.

This was one of those rare cases that got better as the evidence came in. The timing of the walk to the other apartment and back, the improbability of the defendant's story of climbing the tree, the broken vent with his shoe print on it, the fact that somebody had not only drowned Rose but also tried to cover it up with a pretended electrocution, the fact Burke had beaten her several times and the admission of the *will* into evidence, including the conversation between Rose and her neighbor when Rose gave her the will, all combined to convict Burke of Second Degree Murder.

* * * * *

One of St. Paul's leading drug dealers, Lee W was found dead one day in the rear seat of his Cadillac, parked in the airport parking lot. He was a treacherous man in many ways. He had several street dealers working for him and if they failed to come up with the correct amount of change, he would inform police when they were in possession of drugs and thereby get them arrested. Lee died with a total of six gunshot wounds to the head — three which did not penetrate the skull. The bullets simply furrowed along between the skull and the skin. This is not an unknown phenomenon. These three were not fatal, but the other three, which penetrated the skull, were.

Lee had a girlfriend, with whom he lived, who called police on the night he was killed and told them Lee was in grave danger. She urged the police to rescue him, but they were unable to get there in time.

Lee's girlfriend, Becky R, who operated a number of *saunas* and had a vanity license plate with the name MADAM, told police Lee had received a call from his former wife and another old girlfriend. They requested he come to their house to view some clothing they had shoplifted that day and, perhaps, purchase it.

Lee left without money, but while at the ex-wife's house, called Becky R and said, "Help, I'm in trouble." It was for this reason Becky R called the police. As noted, he was found at the airport, a day or two later.

The ex-wife and old girlfriend were hard to find, but a peculiar thing occurred about that time. One Barry L showed up in the office of a Hennepin County Sheriff and started telling him some things about the murder. The sheriff got a friend of his from the Minneapolis Homicide Division involved.

At first, Barry told them where the two guns were. He was never arrested but was released to come and go as he pleased. The cops didn't have to give him the Miranda warning. They went to a stream, which was frozen over, and drilled holes in the ice with an ice-fishing auger. Sure enough, in about three feet of water were the two guns, and the clip for one of them. The sheriff, a very large person, laid on the ice and reached in the water up to his armpit and recovered all the evidence. A forensic examination showed these to be the two guns which fired the shots to Lee's head.

Barry L continued to visit his two officer friends and gradually told the entire story a bit at a time. Lee's ex-wife and girlfriend enticed him over to their place, ostensibly to sell him shoplifted clothes. In truth, they all planned to rob him. When he showed up with no money, they made him call Becky to ask her to bring some money. Instead, he told her he was in trouble and to get help.

They got Lee into his car, where Barry L shot him in the head. They were driving through Roseville, in Ramsey County, when they noticed he wasn't dead, but was still kicking in the back seat. Barry made the ex-wife stop and got out and shot Lee again in the head, with Lee's own gun — a more powerful .38. They then drove to the airport in Hennepin County and parked the car with his body in it.

Finally, the ex-wife and girlfriend surfaced and confirmed much of the story. The girlfriend was not present during the shooting. The ex-wife said she had no idea they were going to kill him when they drove off with him in the car. She said she drove and Barry L shot Lee, without her knowing he would do so. When she was asked what she thought when she heard the gunshots go off in the car she said, "I thought, bye-bye, Lee."

Barry L served several years for the murder.

Lee was laid out at the funeral home in his genuine sable coat and matching hat. Becky explained he always wanted to be buried in them. After the viewing and funeral service, he was taken to Duluth to be interred. Becky went along and, before the burial, insisted she wanted to see him one last time. Everyone tried to put her off, but she became more and more adamant. Sure enough, she was right. Lee's brother had taken the coat and hat, along with his brand-new shoes, before the casket was closed.

Why let it go to waste?

* * * * *

One of the most disturbing cases I ever dealt with concerned a father who cut off his 4-year-old daughter's arm half way between the elbow and wrist. The event occurred one night in the fall of the year, just outside his home in a housing project. He lived there with his wife, the daughter, their two-year-old son and a pet canary.

When the police arrived the little girl was immediately rushed to the hospital where the doctors tried to reattach the arm, but without success. Limb reattachment surgery was in its infancy at that point and the failure rate was much higher than it is today. The father explained his daughter was playing outside and fell against the bumper of a car which cut her arm off. Naturally, the police didn't believe an excuse this flimsy and continued questioning him. Eventually, he admitted he took a butcher knife and cut the arm off.

I was assigned the case and as I prepared for trial, I needed some insight into what might cause someone to commit such an act. To this end, I interviewed his wife, even though I knew at the time I would be unable to use her against a claim of spousal privilege (the law has now been altered to allow such testimony). What unfolded was one of the weirdest episodes ever to reach my ears.

Before the interview, I knew police had executed a search warrant at his home and found a large number of peculiar periodicals. They were mostly small magazines, about the size of *Reader's Digest*. These, however, were devoted to hot rods and women in skimpy bathing suits. Leafing through them, a rather striking fact jumped out of the pages. Many of the women were missing limbs; legs, arms, feet, hands, fingers and other body parts. Many also had tattoos on what was left of their limbs. Moreover, when the photos were examined very carefully, it was apparent they had been very painstakingly altered to depict the deformities and tattoos described.

In interviewing his wife, it became apparent she was unaware of his activities relative to the magazines. I noted a number of scars on her face and asked her how she got them. She said often, while she was sleeping, she would wake up cut and bleeding from the face. Almost invariably there would be some broken glass from a Coke bottle in the bed with them. Her husband would then explain that, probably, the children had broken and bottle and put the glass in bed with them. This occurred four or five times during the marriage and the same explanation accompanied each occasion.

I asked what she knew about his proclivity for tattoos. She explained that if he was ever in a public place and saw a woman with a tattoo, he would become very interested in her and had to be admonished not to stare. I asked if she or her husband had any tattoos and she told me the most bizarre story of all. She explained on the night they were engaged, her husband gave each of them a home-made tattoo. As it was not apparent, I asked where it was and she said he tattooed each of them on the upper, inner thigh. I asked what the tattoo looked like (I didn't really want to see it). She said it was a heart shape and inside the heart were his initials, her initials and the date they were engaged. He left room for the night they were married, when he then added that date to the tattoo.

I inquired how he did this and she explained he took an old style fountain pen and repeatedly jabbed it into the skin and then would lift the filling lever to inject a small amount of ink under the skin. This had to be done many dozens of times in order to create the desired effect of continuous lines as in a professionally done tattoo. He gave himself an identical tattoo on his own upper, inner thigh.

As the interview progressed, I asked if there were any other unusual occurrences of this nature and was told the most unusual story of them all. They had a canary in the house which was usually caged. The defendant often remarked whether a canary would be able to manage if one of its legs were to be cut off. He reminisced over this often, wondering if it could stand, if it could still hop around and what difficulties it might encounter. Sure enough, one morning the canary was missing one of its legs.

As the tale unfolded, it became apparent the wife was just beginning to understand the magnitude of her husband's aberrations. For instance, until then, she had not questioned the mysterious cuts which appeared on her face during the night.

At the time, the most severe crime he could be charged with was maiming. This carried a ten-year sentence. We opted to have him committed as a sexual psychopath, which not only got him treatment, but netted him a longer sentence than his prison term would have ammounted to.

* * * * *

Before serial murderers became more commonplace, we had one come to St. Paul, just at the time I began my career in the County Attorney's office in 1961. A young, single woman who was employed at Catholic Charities was found murdered in her bed when she failed to appear for work one morning. She had been brutally beaten, to the point she was unrecognizable. In addition, she had been raped, as seminal fluid was found inside her vagina. She hadn't an enemy in the world. She had no boyfriends and there were no suspects whatsoever.

The case was solved by a very peculiar quirk. A St. Paul couple visiting Washington DC went to the FBI building. Prominently displayed in the foyer, were the famous "10 Most Wanted" criminals in the United States. They recognized one as their neighbor, and told the guard in the lobby. They also told where he lived and worked at a local SuperAmerica car wash.

Word was relayed to the St. Paul Branch and a local agent went to the car wash and made the arrest. On a hunch, he asked very casually, if the suspect murdered Carol R. Without hesitation, the suspect answered "Yes."

The reason this suspect was on the 10 most wanted, was he was suspected of murdering a young woman in Oregon. He plead guilty and received a life sentence in the Minnesota correctional facility, which translated at that time to about 18 years. Before his trial, he admitted to murdering an Oregon woman, a young girl in Kansas City, Misourri and a young woman in Alabama. In most cases, he raped them post mortem, as he did the woman in St. Paul. After the Minnesota sentence was served, he was sent to one of the other states to commence its sentence.

While incarcerated in Minnesota, he was sent to the University Hospital for psychiatric examination. I was privileged to attend the debriefing session where the case was discussed. He had been conceived during a rape, but his father married his mother before he was born. Shortly after his birth, the father took off and left the mother to live with her own mother.

The grandmother greatly resented the child and all he stood for. She was also a very harsh disciplinarian. She would punish him for the slightest wrongdoing by making him get a hammer from a kitchen drawer and bring it to her. Then he had to stand in front of her and she repeatedly hit him under the chin with the flat side of the hammer while she made him recount his sin. The mother never intervened. She was a weak-kneed individual who, after such punishments were inflicted, would comfort her son and give him a cookie.

Not surprisingly, he grew up with enormous resentment for women. While he was in California, before ever coming to Minnesota, he was committed to a mental institution at Atascadero for a sexual offense. Upon his release, the staff notes contained a phrase that was to be prophetic. It was to the effect the patient has gained little or no insight into his problem and can be expected to continue vicious attacks against women.

* * * * *

The Charles W case was one of the most disturbing I have ever encountered. W was a sexual predator who kidnapped young women, raped and tortured them. In the case I prosecuted, he kidnapped the neice of a prominent polititian, sodomized her and nearly killed her.

He confined his predation to the "Seven Corners" area of Minneapolis, near the University. He had already been sent to prison for one such crime, where he raped and beat a young woman, but was paroled after a few years. Other women disappeared from the area and at least one was found dead. Police suspected him because of the MO. In the case being discussed, he found the victim walking to her Volkswagon parked on Cedar Avenue. He asked for a ride to a place where his car had supposedly stalled. She obliged and, as they drove, each smoked a cigarette.

He directed her to an area in St. Paul known as Hidden Falls, a secluded spot bordering the Mississippi River. There he had her stop the car, made her get out, viciously sodomized her and attacked her with an ice pick. He tried to stab her eyes out, but instead the ice pick went in alongside each eye and traveled under the skin, along her skull, for about three or four inches. It is believed he did this to prevent her from later identifying him. He then knocked out about four of her front teeth and cut her chin, leaving a four inch scar. He also stabbed her in the chest causing one of her lungs to collapse. He left her for dead and drove her car back to the area where he first encountered her.

Miraculously, she survived and managed to crawl up a very steep bank to the road where a passing motorist saw her and took her to the hospital. She was able to make a positive identification of her attacker. Moreover, three of his fingerprints were found on the door of her car, in a position compatible with his having closed the door.

The cigarette butts were obtained from the ashtray and analyzed. This was in the days before DNA analysis was available. About 80 percent of the population can be classified as "secretors." This means their blood type is contained in their other bodily fluids. In this case, both the attacker and the victim were secretors. He had Type O blood and hers was Type B. The two cigarette butts contained one O and one B Type in the trace remains of the saliva deposited on them while being smoked.

Charles W pled guilty to kidnapping and received a 40-year sentence, which was the maximum sentence he could be given under Minnesota law at that time. Additionally, he was adjuged a sexual psychopath which, under Minnesota law, required him to be institutionalized in a security hospital until adjuged to no longer be a danger to the public.

Cases such as this, and some of the others I have illustrated, point out the need, on occasion, for some people to be incarcerated with no hope of parole for their entire life.

AFTERWORD

As I look back on my 34-year career, a few thoughts come to mind, the first being that it is an error to say, "The system isn't working." What we have in the United States today is a not a Criminal Justice System, for there is nothing *systematic* about it. It is much better to think of it as a criminal justice process. Our founding fathers deliberately designed what we do *not* to work well. They'd had it with a system and so built in many protections to avoid what they perceived as problems.

Since that time, and particularly during the "Warren Court" of the 1960's, these protections were greatly expanded, as that court perceived police power as something sinister to be reined in. I had a conversation a few years ago with a Public Defender in which I exclaimed we would have a much safer and, in a sense, a much freer society if we no longer had the Supreme Court decisions on search and seizure, confessions and right to counsel immediately upon arrest. He scoffed and accused me of desiring a police state.

I replied, "Yes, just like the one we had in 1960." This puzzled him and he asked what I was talking about. "Don't you remember the terrible police state we had back in the 60's before this entire line of decisions was pronounced by the Supreme Court? Can't you recall how terrible it was?"

I believe at that point it occurred to him that we didn't have a police state at all, and that a repeal of these decisions would not revisit one upon us. Having lived, and worked within the justice process, under both circumstances, I feel that officers of the law and the court were much more able to provide what the general citizenry desired when our hands weren't tied as they are now.

Some argue that the decisions set forth by the Supreme Court don't really contribute to crime because criminals don't read and understand them. There are really two replies to this: First, even though the average criminal doesn't read and understand his rights, he knows intuitively that the hands of law enforcement are somewhat tied and he can weigh the risk-benefit factor as being more in his favor. Second, police, prosecutors and judges do understand all these rights — they know if they run afoul of these holdings, their cases will be thrown out of court. Thus, they obey the limitations placed upon them and are, therefore, far less effective in deterring crime.

As if this isn't enough red tape to unravel, there is a lack of systematic approach among separate governing agencies, aggrivated by the perennial shortfall of tax dollars.

The various city councils determine how many police officers each city will have and how much funding they will provide for the force. It is the various county boards of commissioners that determine how many assistant county attorneys they will provide and how much funding they will have. Finally, the Legislature determines how many judges there will be and funds the Judiciary Branch of the government. None of these three governing bodies consults each other on these subjects, and there is no central authority to coordinate these activities.

Consequently, at least in the metropolitan areas where the most crime occurs, police produce far more investigations than the county attorneys can handle. County boards are torn between responding to requests by county attorneys for more personnel, and taxpayers who are continuously lamenting their grief about the heavy tax load they must bear. Further, the county attorneys are able to far out-produce the judges assigned to hear cases. Again, the Legislature is torn between the same requests for more judges and the taxpayer response to increased taxes.

The caseload for county attorneys is three cases per week. There is no way in the world anyone can try three cases per week, since it takes (on the average) three days to try any case. Moreover, judges have to be assigned anywhere from 20 to 30 cases per week in order to keep current with the incoming case load — even more of an impossibility. Additionally, every time a lawyer is added, it creates the need for secretarial help and an office with all the related expenses. Add another judge and a courtroom, chambers, a court reporter, bailiff and law clerk must be provided.

While all of this is expensive, bear in mind that overlaying the whole process is the cost of additional prison space needed if we eliminate plea bargaining. Right now, the process relies upon 90% guilty pleas and no more than 10 percent actual trials. If those figures were reversed, the whole house of cards would come crashing down.

There is a very simple solution to this problem. Taxpayers should personally contact the various candidates for the posts of County Commissioner and Legislator and tell them in no uncertain terms that they will not support their candidacy without their solemn promise to raise the taxes needed to do what they want.

That's all it would take, but we all know that's about as likely to occur as a Minnesota winter without snow.

As you can see, I offer few, if any solutions; only food for thought. Better minds than mine are going to have to hit upon the solutions. In the meantime, I suggest everyone try to hold onto a good sense of humor — we're going to need it.

— Paul E. Lindholm